About the Author

Peter Killingley graduated from Durham University in the UK in 1982. He has been teaching English since 2003 and has taught in Europe, North Africa, the Middle East, and Asia. He particularly enjoys teaching exam classes, having first started preparing students for the IELTS exam in 2003. He has a CELTA and a Trinity Diploma and is currently teaching at the Australian Centre for Education (ACE) in Phnom Penh, Cambodia.

About the Editor

Mary Kuder graduated from the University of Minnesota in Minneapolis, Minnesota, USA, in 1982. More recently, in May 2015, she received her Master of Arts in English as a Second Language (MA ESL) from Hamline University in St. Paul, Minnesota, USA. She is the editor and researcher of the Glossary of Compensation and Benefits Terms (WorldatWork, 2002), published with the Library of Congress; and the editor of the eBook *100 Points to Consider before Moving or Retiring in Ecuador* (Crowder, 2013). She has been teaching English since 2013 and has taught in the USA, Ecuador, Cambodia, and Mexico. She is currently teaching English in the United States.

IELTS Scholar:

A Companion Guide for Cambridge IELTS Book 6

Peter Killingley, Author
Mary E. Kuder, Co-Author and Editor

AUSTIN MACAULEY PUBLISHERS™
LONDON • CAMBRIDGE • NEW YORK • SHARJAH

Copyright © Peter Killingley and Mary E. Kuder (2019)

The right of **Peter Killingley** and **Mary E. Kuder** to be identified as author of this work has been asserted by them in accordance with section 77 and 78 of the Copyright, Designs and Patents Act 1988.

All rights reserved. No part of this publication may be reproduced, stored in a retrieval system, or transmitted in any form or by any means, electronic, mechanical, photocopying, recording, or otherwise, without the prior permission of the publishers.

Any person who commits any unauthorised act in relation to this publication may be liable to criminal prosecution and civil claims for damages.

A CIP catalogue record for this title is available from the British Library.

ISBN 9781786938701 (Paperback)
ISBN 9781786938718 (Hardback)
ISBN 9781528952125 (ePub e-book)

www.austinmacauley.com

First Published (2019)
Austin Macauley Publishers Ltd
25 Canada Square
Canary Wharf
London
E14 5LQ

Acknowledgements

The author would like to thank all of his IELTS students for their hard work and invaluable feedback. The author would also like to thank all the students and teachers he has worked with over the years, especially those at ACE, Santhor Mok, Phnom Penh, Cambodia. He would particularly like to thank his editor, Mary Kuder, for her invaluable help and support, without which, this book would not have been possible. He is also grateful to all the people at Cambridge University Press who reviewed this book and provided advice regarding copyright, especially Charlotte Adams.

Table of Contents

Introduction		09
Reading Exam		10
Tips for the reading exam		10
IELTS Academic Reading Exam - Question Types		12
Reading Test One		13
Reading Passage 1	Australia's Sporting Success	13
Reading Passage 2	Delivering the Goods	20
Reading Passage 3	Climate Change and the Inuit	22
Reading Test Two		26
Reading Passage 1	Advantages of Public Transport	26
Reading Passage 2	Greying Population Stays in the Pink	33
Reading Passage 3	Numeration	34
Reading Test Three		41
Reading Passage 1	Early Cinema	41
Reading Passage 2	Motivating Employees under Adverse Conditions	43
Reading Passage 3	The Search for the Anti-aging Pill	47
Reading Test Four		51
Reading Passage 1	Doctoring Sales	51
Reading Passage 2	Do Literate Women make better Mothers?	55
Reading Passage 3	Bullying at School	63
Tips for the listening exam		64
IELTS Academic Listening Exam - Question Types		65
Listening Test One		66
Synonyms and Parallel Expressions		66
Listening Test Two		67
Synonyms and Parallel Expressions		67

Listening Test Three: Synonyms and Parallel Expressions	69
Listening Test Four: Synonyms and Parallel Expressions	71
Tips for the Listening Exam	73
Writing Assessment Criteria	73
Writing Task 1	74
Writing Task 2	75
Tips for the Speaking Exam	76
Speaking Assessment Criteria	77
Answer Keys	79
Reading Test One	79
Reading Passage 1	79
Reading Passage 2	81
Reading Passage 3	83
Reading Test Two	85
Reading Passage 1	85
Reading Passage 2	87
Reading Passage 3	89
Reading Test Three	91
Reading Passage 1	91
Reading Passage 2	93
Reading Passage 3	96
Reading Test Four	98
Reading Passage 1	98
Reading Passage 2	101
Reading Passage 3	103
Listening Test One	107
Listening Test Two	108
Listening Test Three	109
Listening Test Four	110

INTRODUCTION

This book is designed to be used in conjunction with the series of test books of authentic IELTS tests published by Cambridge University Press. It has been designed primarily for students studying for the academic version of the IELTS Exam, but will also be of use to teachers preparing students for that exam. It will also be of use for those students studying for the general version IELTS Exam in that the speaking and listening are the same. However, the writing and reading sections for the general exam will differ from those of the academic exam.

The reading section gives overall advice for this section of the exam and guides the reader through the questions in a systematic fashion. Additionally, there is a vocabulary activity after each section, using vocabulary from the reading itself. A detailed analysis of all the answers to the reading questions can be found at the back of the book. The listening section also gives overall advice on how to approach the exam and highlights the synonyms and parallel expressions that are used. An awareness of these is essential in order to do well in both the listening and the reading exams. You should first do the listening test and then listen to it again to check any answers you got wrong and to complete the synonyms and parallel expressions. An answer key for the synonyms and parallel expressions can also be found at the back of the book.

You should be aware that there are no shortcuts to doing well in the IELTS Exam; students with a low language level will not get a good IELTS score. There is no point doing any kind of IELTS preparation course until a good level of English has been reached, meaning at least at an upper intermediate level.

As well as doing practice tests, you need to think about other ways of improving your English. For example, you should read and listen to as much English as they can to extend your vocabulary. Reading "Easy Readers"at a level one level below your current class level will reinforce knowledge of grammatical structures and vocabulary and ultimately improveyour writing ability. Students who do well in the listening section of the exam tend to be students who watch a wide variety of films in English. Additionally, there is plenty of material available on the internet and in print. A good knowledge of vocabulary is essential to doing well in the exam. For this reason, a copy of the Academic Word List(Coxhead, 2000) would be useful. You should try to learn about ten new words every week that you think would be useful and try to make these words active by incorporating them into your written and spoken English.

The materials in this book have been and are being tested at ACE (Australian Centre for Education) in Cambodia.

Tips for the Reading Exam

In order to do well in the reading test, you should read as much English as possible outside the classroom and expand your vocabulary. The reading texts in the exam are authentic and usually come from magazines, but may also come from books, journals, newspapers, and online resources. Below are a few hints that should help you when you take the reading component of the IELTS Exam. You should "practice" performing these actions when you are taking the practice exams so that these behaviours become automatic long before taking the actual IELTS Exam.

- During the exam, you will not have time to read the article properly before you look at the questions. You should always read the title and any subtitles, however, and skim the text to get a general idea of what it is about and how it is structured. You should not spend more than a minute doing this. You should then look at the questions and try to locate the part of the text where you can find the answers.
- The first questions in each section tend to focus more on the first part of the text while the last questions focus more on the last part of the text. Be careful, however, as this is not always the case.
- Time is your enemy during the exam. If you had two hours to answer the questions, you would do much better. You should spend no more than 20 minutes on each section. You have to answer 40 questions in 60 minutes. That gives you just one and a half minutes per question. Do not waste time on a difficult question. Go on to the next one and go back to any difficult ones at the end.
- The readings are supposed to get progressively more difficult throughout the exam, although this is not always apparent.
- The answers to some questions, such as multiple choice questions and True/False/Not Given or Yes/No/Not Given questions are in the same order as the text. Therefore, when you have answered one question, the answer to the next question will be further along in the text. N.B.: True/False/Not Given questions are associated with factual situations/questions, while Yes/No/Not Given questions are associated with situations in which an opinion is asked for or given.
- Look out for synonyms and paraphrases. Very often, you will not find the same words in the text as in the questions but instead will find synonyms and paraphrases. Sometimes, the word order in the text will be different from the order in the questions; a different part of speech may also be used.
- Use the proper nouns, names, and dates in the questions to help you locate where the answers can be found in the text. Underline the words and read the sentences containing them as well as those before and after them to answer the questions.
- There is almost always at least one "Not Given"/ "Does Not Say" answer for True/False/Not Given or True/False/Does Not Say question. It is possible that there will be

no "Not Given"/"Does Not Say" answer if there is a block of only three questions of that type.
- You will not know all the vocabulary, so you will need to guess the meaning of important words from the context. You do not need to know the meaning of all the words in order to answer the questions correctly.
- Every time you do an IELTS reading, it is a good idea to record the synonyms and parallel expressions in the text that are the same as or similar to those in the questions.
- During the exam, you must transfer your answers onto a separate answer sheet within the exam time; you will not get extra time at the end to do this. Therefore, you should transfer your answers as you go along. If you leave doing this until the end of the exam, you may not have enough time to transfer all of your answers. Be careful, and make sure that you write the correct answer next to the correct question number.
- At the end of the exam, you should check to ensure that you have not left any questions unanswered. If you do not know an answer, just guess! You will not lose any marks for an incorrect answer. If you leave an answer blank, you get no points for that answer. If you guess and answer incorrectly, you get no points for that answer. If you guess and answer correctly, however, you will get points for that answer!
- Pay special attention to "controlling" words in the question, such as "all", "most" and "never".

IELTS Academic Reading Exam Question Types

There are three reading texts in each Reading exam, and a variety of question types.

For the following question types, the answers will always follow the order of the text (e.g., the answer to question five will be found in the text after the information containing the answer to question four, and before the information containing the answer to question six):

1. Matching sentence beginnings and endings
2. *Identifying information* - True/False/Not Given
3. *Identifying the writer's view/claims* - Yes/No/Does Not Say
4. Multiple choice
5. Short answer
6. Sentence completion

The answer to these question types may not follow the order of the text:

7. Summary completion
8. Diagram label completion

The answer to these final question types will not follow the order of the text:

9. Matching information with paragraphs
10. Matching features
11. Matching paragraphs and headings

Test Book 6

Reading Test 1, Reading Passage 1: Australia's Sporting Success

On the reading exam, the words in the questions will often be different from the words in the text, but the meaning will be the same or similar: they use synonyms and paraphrases. Match the words in the questions in column A with the synonyms and paraphrases in the text in column B for Questions 1 to 7.

A	B
(1): visual imaging	(a): finances
(2): reproduced	(b): copying
(3): funded	(c): images from digital cameras
(4): before an event	(d): a number of
(5): different	(e): before a championship

Match the words in the questions in column A with the synonyms and paraphrases in the text in column B for Questions 8 to 11.

A	B
(1): currently	(a): now
(2): in the future	(b): everyone
(3): both Australians and their rivals	(c): will + infinitive* + sbdy + infinitive

*Throughout this book, "infinitive" will refer to the bare infinitive or the base form of the verb, which is sometimes also called form 1 of the verb (v1).

How to Answer Questions 1 to 7:

Questions 1 to 7 are "matching information with paragraphs" questions, and you must find which paragraph contains the information in the question (this is different from "matching paragraphs and headings" questions). In these types of questions, a paragraph may be used as an answer more than once for the same set of questions.

Question 1

Sometimes, key words in the question will be the same as those in the paragraph. In which paragraphs can you find the word "sports"?

"Expertise" means having a great knowledge of something. Which people are experts? In which paragraph are they mentioned?

Underline the key sentence that indicates that expertise is exchanged between different sports.

Question 2

Find the paraphrase for "visualimaging".

Read the sentences before and after the paraphrase to check that it is the correct paragraph.

Question 3

This is a difficult one to find. Try to find a sentence that says why some areas of research are not useful.

Question 4

Proper nouns and the names of organisations will help you to find the correct paragraph. Which paragraphs mention the organisation "AIS"? Unfortunately, the only paragraph that does not mention it is E. Therefore, you can be confident that E is not the correct answer.

Now, find a synonym for "reproduced".

Read more to see if this is the correct paragraph.

Can you guess what "optimum" means?

What factors can affect an athlete's achievement? Think about things like technique and health problems. In which paragraph are they mentioned?

Read carefully to check that it is the correct paragraph.

Question 6

Organisations often fund or pay for things. Which paragraph mentions the names of sporting bodies or organisations?

Read carefully to check that it is the correct paragraph.

Question 7

Find the paraphrase of "before an event".

Read carefully to check that this is the correct paragraph.

How to Answer Questions 8 to 11:

These are classification-type questions that are one type of "matching features" question. Do not write more than one letter for each answer.

Find the words "cameras", "sensors", "protein", and "altitude tent" in the reading passage and underline them. They can be found between the beginning of paragraph C and the end of paragraph F.

Think of ways of saying that sovmething is happening currently and the tenses that will be used. For example, *"currently"* = *"now"*. Also, think about ways of expressing the future using different words than *"in the future"*.

Can you guess what the word "rivals" means?

Now, read around the words you have underlined and answer the questions.

How to Answer Questions 12 and 13:

These are "short answer" questions. The answers to the last set of questions can often be found at the end of the reading. In this test, the answer to question 12 can be found in the penultimate (last but one) paragraph and the answer to question 13 in the last paragraph. To answer the last question, find where it says *"Olympic Games"* and *"1996"*, and read the sentence carefully. NB: It is often necessary to read the sentences before and after the "target sentence", also.

Vocabulary from Test Book 6

Reading Test 1, Reading Passage 1: Australia's Sporting Success

Match the words from the reading in column A with the definitions in column B.

A	B
(1): scope	(a): to pay for something
(2): optimum	(b): to destroy something
(3): to fund	(c): the best possible
(4): to demolish	(d): the range

A	B
(1): altitude	(a): the process of taking food into our bodies and using it
(2): nutritional	(b): to spin or turn from side to side
(3): to swivel	(c): the length of time
(4): duration	(d): the distance (height) above sea level

A	B
(1): extensive	(a): to work with somebody
(2): intensive	(b): covering a large area
(3): to collaborate	(c): covering a small area
(4): a prototype	(d): the first design of something

A	B
(1): velocity	(a): to keep going for a long time
(2): unobtrusive	(b): how often you do something
(3): frequency	(c): speed
(4): endurance	(d): not attracting attention

How to Answer Questions 14 to 17:

These are "matching information" questions. Look at questions 14 to 16, and underline the key words in the questions?

Question 14

Which paragraph often contains a suggestion?
Read the paragraph carefully to see if you are correct.
What words are used to make the suggestion?

Question 15

How are things *"delivered"* electronically? What kind of words should you look for in the text?
Read carefully to see if it is the right paragraph.

Question 16

Can you think of a synonym for the word *"local"*?
"abroad" means in another country. Which paragraphs mention the names of other countries?

Question 17

Can you find a paraphrase of *"the value of goods"*?
Read carefully to see if it is the right paragraph

How to Answer Questions 18 to 22:

These are "identifying information" questions. True/False/Not Given questions are in the same order as the text. There is almost always at least one question for which "Not Given" is the answer.

Question 18

The first answer can be found in paragraph A. In the question, the words are *"world economy"*, whereas in text they are *"global economy"*. Remember, the words in the question will often be different from the words in the text, but the meaning will be the same. *"Increasing"* is found in the question but *"expanding"* is found in the text.
The key sentence is, *"While the global economy has been expanding at a bit over 3% a year, the volume of trade has been rising at a compound annual rate of about twice that."* What is the correct answer?

Question 19

Sometimes, the words in the question will be the same as the words in the text. Find the words *"cheap labour"* in the text.

The key sentence is, *"Cheap labour may make Chinese clothing competitive in America, but if delays in shipments tie up working capital and cause winter coats to arrive in spring, trade may lose its advantages."* What is the correct answer?

Question 20

Proper nouns such as the names of countries will be the same in the question as in the text. Find the words *"France"* and *"Japan"* in the text. Read carefully. What is the correct answer?

Question 21

In the question, the words are *"nearby nations"* whereas in the text they are *"geographic neighbours"*. Find the words *"geographic neighbours"* in the text.

The key sentence is, *"Countries still trade disproportionately with their geographic neighbours."* What is the correct answer?

Question 22

Can you find the word *"Germany"* further in the text?
Neither can I. What is the correct answer?

How to Answer Questions 23 to 26:

This is a "summary-completion" question, where the words you need to use are in a box below the summary. The answers will be found in a small part of the text. As they are the last questions for this section of the reading, they will probably be found in the latter part of the text.

You should read through the summary first, to try to make sense of it and to predict the types of words that are missing. In this case, all the words are either plural or uncountable nouns, so any word would fit grammatically into any gap.

Do not forget that the words in the box may be different from the words in the text, but the meaning will be the same. For example, a "disc drive" is a part of a computer. A "part" is another word for a "component".

Do not worry if you find this particular set of questions difficult. It is. However, do not forget to answer all the questions in the exam: so if you do not know a particular answer, just guess! Then, read through the summary to see if it makes sense.

Vocabulary from Test Book 6
Reading Test 1, Reading Passage 2: Delivering the Goods

Match the words in column A with their synonyms or definitions in column B. They are from the IELTS reading. Remember to make a note of new words when you have done an IELTS reading. Try to learn any words that you think will be useful.

A	B
(1): startling	(a): unimportant
(2): insignificant	(b): a limit on the quantity of something
(3): customs duties	(c): a tax on imports
(4): a quota	(d): amazing

A	B
(1): minor	(a): small or unimportant
(2): instantly	(b): business
(3): friction	(c): immediately
(4): commerce	(d): when something cannot move easily

A	B
(1): processed	(a): large, taking up a lot of space
(2): bulky	(b): manufactured
(3): a restriction	(c): a tax on imports
(4): to dominate	(d): amazing

A	B
(1): an obstacle	(a): a thing that makes progress difficult
(2): to shift	(b): to change something dramatically
(3): swift	(c): quick
(4): to transform	(d): to move

Test Book 6

Reading Test 1, Reading Passage 3: Climate Change and the Inuit
How to Answer Questions 27 to 33:

In these"matching paragraphs and headings"questions, you need to find out what the main idea of the paragraph is. One way of doing this is to read one paragraph at a time and to think of your own heading. Then, look at the list of headings and see if any are similar.

To save time, you can often get the answer from the topic sentence. This is often, but not always, the first sentence of the paragraph. The last sentence of a paragraph is also useful as it is sometimes a summary of the paragraph. However, you will need to look at the whole paragraph to check that you are right. In this reading, you can get many of the answers from the topic sentences. Nonetheless, be careful, especially with paragraph D.

Answer the questions you are most sure about first, as if you use an answer you are not sure of, you eliminate it as a possible answer for the other questions. By doing so, you may eliminate an answer for another question that it IS the correct answer for. Therefore, as you answer this type of question, always check any headings you have already used, as they may be a better fit for the paragraph you are currently looking at than they are for the one you have already used it for.

Always cross out the heading used as an answer in the example before you start, so you do not use it by mistake.

A	B
(1): impossible	(a): the food you need to survive
(2): sustenance	(b): to cope
(3): to be successful	(c): to rely on
(4): a few	(d): a handful
(5): to give something up	(e): out of the question
(6): to depend on	(f): to abandon something

Vocabulary from Test Book 6

Reading Test 1, Reading Passage 3: Climate Change and the Inuit

Remember to check the definition of any words you think might be useful when you have done an IELTS reading. It is a great way of increasing your vocabulary. Try to learn the words that you think will be useful.

Match the words in column A with their synonyms or definitions in column B.

A	B
(1): to thaw	(a): to protect something from heat, cold, or sound
(2): an igloo	(b): rainfall
(3): to insulate	(c): a house made of ice
(4): precipitation	(d): to melt

A	B
(1): precarious	(a): not safe
(2): ancestors	(b): independence
(3): content (adj.)	(c): people related to us who are dead
(4): autonomy	(d): happy

A	B
(1): terrain	(a): expensive
(2): a threat	(b): always living in different places
(3): nomadic	(c): a danger
(4): costly	(d): landscape

A	B
(1): precarious	(a): when you are unhappy
(2): ancestors	(b): believable
(3): content (adj.)	(c): a worry
(4): autonomy	(d): to affect

Test Book 6

Reading Test 2, Reading Passage 1: Advantages of Public Transport

How to Answer Questions 1 to 5:

In these "matching paragraphs and headings" questions, the topic sentence will sometimes help you. This is often, but not always, the first sentence. In this particular test, you will need to read the paragraphs carefully as the first sentence, on its own, will not give you the answer. Occasionally, the last sentence in a paragraph summarises the main idea.

Look out for paraphrasing and synonyms, as the words in the text will often be different from the words in the headings. The meanings, however, will be similar.

Match the words and phrase from the text in Column A with synonyms and paraphrases from the headings in Column B.

A	B
(1): commutin	(a): increases
(2): far higher	(b): higher incomes
(3): increasing wealth	(c): travelling

Question 1 (paragraph A)

The important words in this paragraph are *"democratic"* and *"referendum"*.

Question 2 (paragraph B)

In this paragraph, the last sentence is the key sentence. The key word is *"commuting"*.

Question 3 (paragraph C)

In this paragraph, the first two sentences are the important sentences. The key word is "refutes". To refute something is to prove that something is not true.

Question 4 (paragraph D)

Sometimes, In this paragraph, the second sentence is the most important. What would happen if everyone lived in the city centre?

Question 5 (paragraph D)

In this paragraph, the last sentence is the key sentence.

How to Answer Questions 6 to 10:

These are "identifying information - True/False/Not Given" questions, and the questions follow the order of the text. Proper nouns and initials, such as "ISTP" and "Melbourne", will help you to locate the answers in the text. You will not need to read all the text to find the answers -- just a part of it. As you have already answered questions on the last five paragraphs, it is likely that the answers to the remaining questions will be found mostly in the rest of the text.

Question 6

The answer to the first question is in the first paragraph. How many cities did the study examine? How many cities are there in the world?

Question 7

The answer to the second question is in the second paragraph. Read what it says about "efficient cities". Is it the same as or different from this statement?

Question 8

The answer to this question is in the third paragraph. Read the third sentence about Melbourne's large tram network and answer the question.

Question 9

The answer to this question is in the last sentence of paragraph three. Read it and answer the question.

Question 10

The answer to this question is in paragraph five.

How to Answer Questions 11 to 13:

Although synonyms and paraphrases are normally used in these types of questions, sometimes you will find the same words in the text as in the questions, or you may find words, or phrases with an opposite meaning. For example, "**hilly**", "road" and "**light rail**" are all in the text and the questions. On the other hand, in one of the questions, the word "inefficient" is used, but in the text the opposite phrase "**more efficient**" can be found."``

Vocabulary from Test Book 6

Reading Test 2, Reading Passage 1: Advantages of Public Transport

Match the words from the text in column A with their synonyms or definitions in column B.

A	B
(1): to demonstrate	(a): the least amount possible
(2): minimal	(b): a sudden increase
(3): the suburbs	(c): the outer parts of a city
(4): an explosion	(d): to show how somthing works

A	B
(1): inadequate	(a): not enough
(2): reasonable	(b): groups of people who put pressure on the goverment to chagne the law
(3): an objection	(c): not bad but not good
(4): lobbies	(d): an expression of disapproval

A	B
(1): a referendum	(a): amazing
(2): spectacular	(b): at the beginning
(3): to be stable	(c): to remain the same
(4): intially	(d): to vote by all the people

A	B
(1): infrastructure	(a): possible
(2): congestion	(b): the basic things a society needs such as roads, bridges and power supplies
(3): viable	(c): not bad but not good
(4): to disperse	(d): an expression of disapproval

Test Book 6

Reading Test 2, Reading Passage 1: Advantages of Public Transport

Before you look at the questions, you should have a quick glance at the reading passage to see what it is about. Headings and sub-headings will help you. Look at the heading. Can you guess what the article is about?

How to Answer Questions 14 to 22:

These are "summary completion" questions, and the words that you need to use are in a box below the summary. The first thing you should do is read the summary to make sense of it. You should also predict the types of words that are missing. You should then look at the text to find the answers. The summary will usually only relate to a part of the text. As these are the first questions for this part of the reading, it is likely that the summary will relate to the first part of the text. In fact, the summary relates to the first seven paragraphs. Do not forget to look for synonyms and paraphrasing, as the words in the text are not normally the same as in the question.

Predicting what words are missing

Question 14

What type of word can come after "**is**"?

The article talks about a change. What tense do you use for a changing situation? Hint: You are looking for a present participle. How many are there in the box?

Check the reading (paragraph 1) to see which is the correct answer.

Question 15

This will also be a present participle. There is only one left in the box.

Check the reading (paragraph 2) to make sure that the answer is correct.

Question 16

What type of word normally goes before "than"? Hint: You are looking for a comparative adjective.

There are two comparative adjectives in the box. Read paragraph three to see which one is correct.

Question 17

"in" is a preposition. What type of word follows a preposition? Hint: There is no article, so it must be a plural or uncountable noun.

There are six uncountable nouns in the box. The first sentence in paragraph four will give you the answer.

Question 18

"improved" is an adjective. What type of word normally comes after an adjective?

The answer can be found in the last sentence in paragraph four.

Question 19

In this sentence "to" is a preposition. What type of word comes after a preposition?

Paragraph five will give you the answer.

Question 20

"of" is a preposition, so you need to use a noun.

Paragraph six will give you the answer.

Question 21

What type of word normally comes after "are"? Hint: You are looking for an adjective.

You can find the answer in paragraph seven.

Question 22

What type of word comes after "the"?

You can find the answer in the last sentence of paragraph seven.

A	B
(1): poorer air quality	(a): increasing
(2): medical advances	(b): age-related medical problems
(3): a financial burden	(c): speed
(4): diseases associated with old age	(d): medicine
(5): a correlation	(e): improved
(6): improvements in	(f): pollution
(7): fewer and fewer	(g): life expectancy
(8): a significant drop	(h): cost
(9): live an extra seven years	(i): a significant reduction
(10): rate	(j): falling
(11): accelerate	(k): a link

How to Answer Questions 23 to 26:

These are "sentence completion" questions. As they are the last questions in this section, they are likely to relate to the last part of the reading. In fact, the answers can be found in the last five paragraphs.

Some words in the question might be the same as in the reading. Find the words "**home medical aids**" in the reading and underline them. Other words may be paraphrased. Find the expressions "**daily physical activity**", "**felt in control of their lives**", and "**emotionally isolated**" and underline them. These phrases have the same meaning as the phrases in questions 24 to 26. Now, read the text around these phrases carefully and complete the sentences using your own words. Then, match them with the answers.

Vocabulary from Test Book 6

Reading Test 2, Reading Passage 2: Greying Population Stays in the Pink

Match the words from the text in column A with their synonyms or definitions in column B.

A	B
(1): elderly	(a): to increase quickly
(2): associated with	(b): affecting badly
(3): afflicting	(c): related to
(4): to accelerate	(d): old

A	B
(1): dementia	(a): a disease affecting your memory
(2): predecessors	(b): a sudden increase
(3): a surge	(c): not obvious
(4): subtle	(d): people who came before

A	B
(1): complex	(a): not simple
(2): a burden	(b): very big
(3): massive	(c): to get worse
(4): to deteriorate	(d): a problem

A	B
(1): an epidemiologist	(a): an exercise machine you walk on
(2): a drawback	(b): a disadvantage
(3): to underestimate	(c): a person who studies diseases
(4): a treadmill	(d): to think that something is less than it really is

Test Book 6 – Reading Test 2, Reading Passage 3: Numeration

Often the first questions in the reading will relate more to the first part of the text, and the last questions to the end of the text. However, that is not the case with this reading. Questions 27 to 31 relate to paragraphs two to six, and questions 32 to 40 relate to paragraphs two to seven.

How to Answer Questions 27 to 31:

In these types of questions ("sentence completion" questions), the questions are in the same order as the text. You need to locate where the information is in the text, and read the information carefully. Try to complete the sentence in your own words before you match it with the options.

If you can find a proper noun in the question, this should be easy to locate in the text. Question 29 mentions "**seventh-century Europe**". Locate it in the text and underline it. The answers to questions 27 and 28 will come before it, and questions 30 and 31 will come after it.

Normally, the words and expressions in the questions will be different from the words and expressions in the reading, but the meaning will be the same or similar. Sometimes, the words will be the same or almost the same. This is the case for question 31, where the words in the question are "**according to the class of item**" and in the text they are "**according to the class of the item**" (paragraph six, line three).

For questions 27 to 30, match the expressions in the questions with those in the text. Now, match the

expressions in column A with those in column B.

A	B
(1): dementia	(a): a disease affecting your memory
(2): predecessors	(b): a sudden increase
(3): a surge	(c): not obvious
(4): subtle	(d): people who came before

Now, find the expressions in column B in the text, and read the information around them carefully. Try to complete the sentences in your own words, and then match them to the correct endings A to G in the exam.

How to Answer Questions 32 to 40:

"Identifying information - True/False/Not Given" questions are in the same order as the text. Read the statements 32 to 40, and underline the key words in the text, especially any proper nouns, as these will often be the same in the text. It is often possible to find the same words in the text as in the questions. If you can do this, it will help you to locate where the answers are. Underline the key words in the text, and then read the sentences around them carefully and decide what the answer is.

Below is a list of key words in the questions that can also be found in the text. Find and underline the words in the text, and answer the questions.

Question 32
"earliest tribes"

Question 33
"indigenous Tasmanians"

Question 34
There are no words that are the same for this question, but you know that the answer will be found in the text, between the answers for questions 33 and 35.

Question 35
"cultures"

Question 36
"Anglo-Saxon"

Question 37
"seventh-century Europe"

Question 38
"the Tsimshian language"

Question 39
"the Tsimshian language"

Question 40
"fingers"/"pebbles"

The easiest words to find will probably be "**indigenous Tasmanians**". If you can find these words, you know that the answer to question 32 will come before them and the answers to the other questions will come after them.

Vocabulary from Test Book 6

Reading Test 2, Reading Passage 3: Numeration

Match the words from the reading in column A with their synonyms or definitions in column B. Remember to make a note of any new words when you have done an IELTS reading and try to remember the most useful ones.

A	B
(1): a feat	(a): a strong belief
(2): a facility	(b): a thought
(3): a consideration	(c): the ability to do something
(4): a conviction	(d): an achievement

A	B
(1): sufficient	(a): enough
(2): to reflect on	(b): not simple
(3): sophisticated	(c): of the highest importance
(4): paramount	(d): to think about

A	B
(1): indigenous	(a): hand signals
(2): gestures	(b): to be enough
(3): to suffice	(c): native
(4): fundamental	(d): basic

A	B
(1): distinct	(a): something that makes something else difficult to do
(2): a hindrance	(b): separate
(3): the relics	(c): an idea
(4): a concept	(d): the remains

Vocabulary from Test Book 6
Reading Test 1, Reading Passage 3: Climate Change and the Inuit
How to Answer Questions 27 to 31:

For questions 1 to 5, you have to find which paragraph contains the information in the questions for these "matching information with paragraphs" questions. These are not the same as the "matching paragraphs and headings" questions.

Sometimes, you will find the same words in the text as in the questions. For example, in question 2, the word **"stories"** is in both the question and in the text. More often, however, you will need to find synonyms and paraphrases. Think of other ways of expressing the following words from the questions: **"location"**; **"speed"**; **"teaches us"**; **"other cultures"**; **"actors in films"**.

The best way to approach this task is to read the statements first and then read one paragraph at a time to see if it contains information from any of the headings, looking out for synonyms and parallel expressions of words in the statements.

Match the words and phrases from the questions in column A with their synonyms or paraphrases from the text in column B.

A	B
(1): the location	(a): enough
(2): the speed	(b): not simple
(3): teaches us	(c): of the highest importance
(4): other cultures	(d): to think about
(5): actors in films	(f): 14 Boulevard des Capucines in Paris

Now, answer questions 1 to 5.

How to Answer Questions 6 to 9:

"Identifying information - Yes/No/Not Given" questions will always follow the order of the text. Proper nouns such as the names of places, people, and organisations are useful, as they will be the same in the question and the text. As a result, they will help you to locate where the answers are in the text. In question 7 you can see the words "Lumiere Brothers". Find these words in the text and underline them. The answer to question 7 is in paragraph C. You now know that the answer to question 6 will come before this in the text and the answers to questions 8 and 9 afterward.

There is nearly always at least one answer that is "Not Given". Once again, look for synonyms and paraphrases (i.e. "in very early cinema" = "at first").

Think carefully about the information in the text before you answer the question. For example, in question 7, Andrei Tarkovsky thinks that the film was a "work of genius", but what does the writer think? Is this mentioned in the text?

How to Answer Questions 10 to 13:

"Multiple choice" questions are also in the same order as in the text. Once again, proper nouns will help you to find where the answers are in the text. In question 11, you can see the name "Tarkovsky". Find and underline the name "Tarkovsky" in the text. You can see that it is mentioned twice (in paragraph C and in paragraph D). In one paragraph, you learn of his opinion about a particular film, while in the other you find out about what he thinks of cinema in general. It is his opinion about cinema in general that is important for this question. In which paragraph can you find this? The answer to question 10 will be found before this, and the answers to questions 12 and 13 will come after it.

It might be a good idea to answer the question before you look at options A, B, C and D. You can then match your answer with one of the options.

Now, answer questions 10 to 13.

Test Book 6

Reading Test 3, Reading Passage 1: Early Cinema

Match the words and phrases from the text in column A with their definitions in column B.

A	B
(1): stunned	(a): only
(2): thrilled	(b): very excited
(3): dynamic	(c): shocked
(4): mere	(d): always changing

A	B
(1): to dominate	(a): very closely
(2): intimately	(b): 100% certain to happen
(3): inevitably	(c): to suggest that something is true
(4): to imply	(d): to have complete control or power over something or somebody

A	B
(1): enduring	(a): something that is interesting because it is new
(2): a legacy	(b): lasting for a long time
(3): a novelty	(c): something you leave behind when you go
(4): a gimmick	(d): a trick or device intended to attract attention

A	B
(1): overwhelmingly	(a): a story
(2): a narrative	(b): amazing
(3): fled	(c): ran away
(4): astonishing	(d): mostly

Test Book 6

Reading Test 3, Reading Passage 2: Motivating Employees under Adverse Conditions

How to Answer Questions 14 to 18:

These are "matching paragraphs and headings" questions, so you need to find the main idea of each paragraph and match it to an appropriate heading. Sometimes, you need to read the whole paragraph in order to be able to do this. One idea is to think of your own heading, and match it to one of the headings in the question.

Occasionally, but not always, you can get the answer from the topic sentence of each paragraph, without reading the entire paragraph. The topic sentence is often, but not always, the first sentence in the paragraph. In this particular reading, it is possible to match all the paragraphs with the correct heading just by reading the first sentence of each paragraph. This is unusual.

Do not forget to look for synonyms and paraphrases as the words in the questions are not usually exactly the same as in the reading.

Before you start, you should put a line through the answer used for the example (viii) so that you do not use it by mistake. Now, answer questions 14 to 18.

Match the words and phrases in the questions in column A with the words and phrases in the text in column B. This will help you to check your answers. Some words, such as "rewards", are the same in the question and the answer.

A	B
(1): give feedback	(a): equitable/equal
(2): link	(b): achievable
(3): a reward	(c): goals
(4): targets	(d): contingent
(6): trealistic	(e): receive comments on how well they are doing
(5): fair	(f): a reinforcement

43

How to Answer Questions 19 to 24:

In these types of questions ("identifying information -Yes/No/Not Given" questions), the questions will be in the same order as the text. Sometimes, the words will be the same in the text and in the question, but often you will need to look for synonyms and paraphrases. Normally, at least one answer will be "Not Given".

Question 19

The first question might be near the beginning of the text. In this question, the word **"shrinking"** is the same in the question and the text. Find it in the first paragraph and underline it. Now, read the information around it, and answer the question. Is the word "minor" more likely to refer to less skilled or more skilled employees?

Question 20

The words **"small business"** can be found in the text. Find them and underline them in Key Point One. Read the words before and after it carefully, and answer the question.

Question 21

The answer to this question will be later in the text. Find and underline the words **"high achievers"** in the text. Read the information carefully. Is the word "independence" the same as or the opposite of "team work"?

Question 22

Sometimes, the word in the question is a different part of speech from the word in the text. In this case, there are the words **"manipulated"** and **"manipulative"**. Find the word "manipulative" and answer the question. You do not need to know what the word means in order to be able to answer the question.

Question 23 and 24

Now, answer questions 23 and 24. The important synonyms and paraphrases here are **"earnings" = "rewards"**, and **"transparent" = "disclosed to everyone"**.

How to Answer Questions 19 to 24:

For these "matching features" questions, you need to find and underline the words in the questions in the text. Find and underline the words "high achievers", "clerical workers", and "production workers".

Now, look at the descriptions, and underline the key words in each description.

Next, read the information carefully, and match each with ONE of the descriptions. Do not write more than one letter for each answer. You will not use two of the letter answers. Some words might be the same in the descriptions and the text. Here, "external goals" and "quality of work" are in the descriptions and the texts.

For other words, you will need to look for synonyms and paraphrases. When you have found the answers, check them by matching the paraphrases and synonyms from the descriptions in column A with the text in column B, below.

A	B
(1): less need	(a): advancement
(2): important	(b): near the top of their list
(3): promotion	(c): rated very highly
(4): important	(d): less important

Test Book 6

Reading Test 3, Reading Passage 1: Early Cinema

Match the words and phrases from the text in column A with their definitions in column B.

A	B
(1): to motivate	(a): getting bigger
(2): expanding	(b): constantly changing
(3): dynamic	(c): getting smaller
(4): shrinking	(d): to provide someone with a reason for doing something

A	B
(1): made redundant	(a): a large amount, plenty
(2): an abundance	(b): lost their job
(3): affiliation	(c): in cooperation with
(4): in conjunction with	(d): belonging

A	B
(1): manipulative	(a): views
(2): perceptions	(b): judgement
(3): appraisal	(c): independence
(4): autonomy	(d): to get someone to do what you want them to do

A	B
(1): scope	(a): range
(2): remuneration	(b): obvious, clear
(3): transparent	(c): an office worker
(4): a clerical worker	(d): pay

Test Book 6

Reading Test 3, Reading Passage 3: The Search for the Anti-aging Pill

How to Answer Questions 28 to 32:

Often (but not always), the first questions in a text will relate to the first part of the text and the last questions to the latter part of the text. This is true of this particular test, so you need to focus on the first three paragraphs for the first five questions. "Identifying information - Yes/No/Not Given" questions are always in the same order as in the text and there is almost always at least one answer which is "Not Given".

You should look in the text for synonyms and paraphrases of words in the questions. Sometimes, however, you need to look for a word or expression that has an opposite meaning. For Example, in question 32 the phrase is "led shorter lives", whereas the key phrase in the text is "lived longer". For question 30, "harsh", in the text, has an opposite meaning to the word "attractive" in the question. Occasionally, the word in the question will be the same as the word in the text (for example, in question 32, the word "rats" is the same in the question and in the text), because it would be impossible to use a different word without changing its meaning.

To make this task easier for questions 28 to 32, listed below is the sentence in the text where the answer can be found.

Question 28

The first sentence of the first paragraph

Question 29

The last sentence of the first paragraph

Question 30

The second sentence of the second paragraph

Question 31

The middle of the second paragraph (Obviously, diseases are more common among older people, but is this because of their diet?)

Question 32

The second sentence of the third paragraph

Answer questions 28 to 32. When you have finished, match the words in column A with their synonym or paraphrase in column B, below, to help check your answers.

A	B
(1): drugs available today	(a): age-related
(2): extend human life	(b): findings
(3): evidence	(c): increase longevity
(4): in older people	(d): treatment on the market today

How to Answer Questions 33 to 37:

In this classification task (which is a type of "matching features" question), you need to find the key words in A, B, and C in the text and underline them. These words are "caloric-restricted" and "control". Find them in the text in paragraphs five and six and underline them.

Now, read the paragraphs carefully and answer questions 33 to 37. Remember to look for synonyms, paraphrases and opposites. For example, question 37 contains the word "greater", whereas the opposite word, "lower", appears in the text. To help check your answers, match the words in column A with their synonyms, paraphrases, or opposites in column B.

A	B
(1): less need	(a) higher
(2): important	(b) decreased likelihood
(3): promotion	(c) reduced risk
(4): important	(d) more

How to Answer Questions 38 to 40:

Questions 38 to 40 require you to label a diagram and are examples of "diagram label completion" questions. Look at the key words in the question. They are, "**caloric-restriction memetic**". Find them in the text and underline them. The answers to these questions can be found in the last two paragraphs of the text. Now, read the two paragraphs carefully, and answer the questions.

Question 38

The word in the question is "**less**". The key words in the text are "**prevents most of it**".

Question 39

There are two theories. Look for "signpost" words to help you find each theory. The first theory is signposted by the words "one possibility". You might also need to find what words pronouns refer to. In the phrase "limit their production", what does "their" refer to?

Question 40

How is the second theory signposted? It is signposted with the words "**another hypothesis**". The synonym for "focus on" in the text is "**emphasizes**".

Test Book 6

Reading Test 3, Reading Passage 3: The Search for the Anti-aging Pill

Match the words from the reading in column A with their synonyms or definitions in column B.

A	B
(1): vulnerability	(a): wide
(2): infirmity	(b): likely to be affected by something
(3): broad	(c): a limit
(4): a restriction	(d): lack of good health

A	B
(1) a mortal	(a) to put off until a later date
(2) equivalent	(b) a routine
(3) a regimen	(c) the same as
(4) to postpone	(d) someone who will eventually die

A	B
(1) an incidence	(a) the existence of something
(2) to retain	(b) serious and long lasting
(3) chronic	(c) basic
(4) fundamental	(d) to keep

A	B
(1) in abundance	(a) to delay the progress of something
(2) to retard	(b) to move
(3) to shift	(c) rare, not common
(4) scarce	(d) a large number or amount

Test Book 6

Reading Test 4, Reading Passage 1: Doctoring Sales

How to Answer Questions 1 to 7:

These are "matching paragraphs and headings" questions. Sometimes, you can get the answer by reading the first sentence of each paragraph, which is often -- but not always -- the topic sentence. It is not possible to do this in this particular example. Other times, you need to read the whole paragraph to get the main idea.

Think of your own heading for the paragraph and try to match it to a heading in the questions. Look for synonyms and paraphrases of words and phrases in the questions in the text.

Occasionally, the last sentence in the paragraph will give a summary of the paragraph. In this particular test, you can get most, but not all, of the answers from the final sentence.

Answer questions 1 to 7. When you have finished, match the words and phrases from the questions in

column A with the words and phrases from the text in column B, below. These are all key words. This will help you to check if your answers are correct.

A	B
(1): financial	(a) much needed/a tremendous advantage
(2): responsible	(b) affected what physicians prescribe
(5): research	(c) not influenced
(3): positive side	(d) to blame/responsibility
(4): not.......persuaded	(e) patients are the ones who pay
(6): promotion works	(f) $200
(7): who really pays	(g) studies

How to Answer Questions 8 to 13:

For theseidentifying information - Yes/No/Not Given" questions, the answers are in the same order as the text. When you have found the answer to the first question, the answer to the second question will be further down the text.

There is almost always at least one answer that is "Not Given".

Try to find any proper nouns in the questions (such as peoples' names, the names of countries, or the names of organisations), as these will help you to locate where the answers are in the text. In this particular example, find the name "**Shaefer**" in the text and underline it.

Next, answer questions 8 to 13. Then, check your answers by looking at the information below.

Question 8

The name "**Shaefer**" appears more than once in the text. The key information for this question is in paragraph B. Are the following phrases the same or different?

Question 8

The name "**Shaefer**" appears more than once in the text. The key information for this question is in paragraph B. Are the following phrases the same or different?

a very limited budget	a budget that could buy lunches and dinners for a small country	same
		different

Question 9

The answer to this question can be found in paragraph C. Are the words below the same or different?

moral	ethical	same
		different

Question 10

The answer to this question can be found in paragraph D. Are the phrases below the same or different?

a very limited budget	a budget that could buy lunches and dinners for a small country	same
		different

Question 11
The answer to this question is in paragraph E. You need to read the whole paragraph.

Question 12
The answer to this question is in paragraph E. You need to read the whole paragraph.

Question 12
The answer to this question is in paragraph E. You need to read the whole paragraph.

		same
a very limited budget	a budget that could buy lunches and dinners for a small country	
		different

Vocabulary from Test Book 6

Reading Test 4, Reading Passage 1: Doctoring Sales

Match the words and phrases from the text in column A with their definitions in column B.

A	B
(1): pharmaceutical	(a): connected with drugs
(2): a physician	(b): normal
(3): typical	(c): a clever device
(4): a gadget	(d): a doctor

A	B
(1): a budget	(a): moral, what is right and wrong
(2): ethical	(b): to pay money illegally
(3): to bribe	(c): increasing
(4): escalating	(d): the amount of money you have to spend on something

A	B
(1): extravagance	(a): to spend more money tha you need to
(2): tremendous	(b): to pay money illegally
(3): an inundation	(c): increasing
(4): the recipient	(d): very large/good

A	B
(1): rocketing	(a): complete/detailed
(2): comprehensive	(b): to check something carefully
(3): to grapple	(c): to try to do something that is difficult
(4): to scrutinize	(d): very large/good

Test Book 6

Reading Test 4, Reading Passage 2: Do Literate Women make better Mothers?

How to Answer Questions 1 to 7:

Sometimes, the questions will follow roughly the same order as the text: the first set of questions will relate to the first part of the text; the second set of questions to the second part of the text; and the last set of questions to the final part of the text. This is the case for this reading. Be careful, though, as this is not always the case. Here, however, questions 14 to 18 relate to paragraphs one to three, questions 19 to 24 relate to paragraphs four to six, and questions 25 to 26 relate to paragraphs seven to nine.

How to Answer Questions 14 to 18:

This is a "summary completion" question where you have to complete the summary from the words in the box underneath. Remember that the summary will focus on just a part of the text; which part is what you will need to find.

Read the summary first so that you understand it and predict the types of words that are missing. In this particular example, all the words are nouns, so it will not help you much. Use any proper nouns, such as "the Nicaraguan National Literacy Crusade", to help you find where the information is in the text.

Read the instructions very carefully. It says that you can use each letter more than once. In this test, you do need to use one letter twice.

Question 14

Here, are you looking for a singular noun, an uncountable noun or a plural noun? Hint: What comes after **"large numbers of"**? There are only two possible answers. Look at the text to find the correct answer; find where it says **"the Nicaraguan National Literacy Crusade"** in the text. Who learnt to **"read, write, and use numbers"**? Was it adults and children, or just adults? What is the correct answer, G or B?

Question 15
Occasionally, you can find the same word in the text as in the question. Find the word "experts"in the first paragraph. Which word in the second sentence means "for many years"? Sometimes, a reference word will refer back to a previous sentence. What does "this idea"refer back to? What makes children healthier? You need to work out or know that "maternal" refers to mothers and "paternal" to fathers, and that "literacy" is the ability to read and write.

Question 16
You can find the answer to this question in paragraph four. What is another word for an academic who investigates something? Do the organisations come from one country or more than one country?

Question 17
Find the word "eliminated"in the text. What do "these factors"refer to? One is "attitudes to children" ("it values its children more highly"). What is the other factor?

Question 18
Find the word "survival"in paragraph one. Another word for an "infant" is a "child". What improves a child's chances of survival?

How to Answer Questions 1 to 7:

The answers to these "identifying information - True/False/Not Given" questions are in the same order as the text. There is nearly always at least one answer that is "Not Given". All the answers can be found in paragraphs four to six.

Question 19
Look at paragraph four. Do you know how many women were interviewed? Do you know how many of the women who were interviewed had learnt to write when they were children?

Question 20
In what year did the Literacy Crusade start? What time expression in paragraph five refers to a time just before this? At this time, the infant mortality rate for illiterate mothers was about 110 per thousand. What was it for women educated in primary school? Is it the same or different?

Question 21
The answer to this question can be found in paragraph six. Find a synonym or antonym for the words "stayed at".

Question 22
The answer to this question can also be found in paragraph six.

Question 23
In paragraph six, you can see that the women who had learnt to read had a rate of 84 per thousand. In paragraph five, you can see the rate for women educated at primary school. Which is lower?

Question 24
In paragraph six, you can see that the children of illiterate women were not as well nourished as the children of the newly-literate mothers. Does this mean they were malnourished? (Hint: If you are malnourished, it means you do not get enough food to eat.)

How to Answer Questions 25 to 26:

The answers to these "multiple choice" questions can be found in paragraphs eight and nine. Which answer can be seen to be wrong by reading paragraph ten? If you find that an option is wrong, cross it out.

Vocabulary from Test Book 6

Reading Test 4, Reading Passage 2: Do Literate Women make better Mothers?

Match the words and phrases from the text in column A with their definitions in column B.

A	B
(1): to survive	(a): to think something is important
(2): literate	(b): to get rid of
(3): to value	(c): able to read and write
(4): to eliminate	(d): not to die

A	B
(1): to remain	(a): complete/detailed
(2): maternal	(b): to check something carefully
(3): paternal	(c): to try to do something that is
(4): mortality	(d): increasing quickly

A	B
(1) autonomous	(a) when things are clean
(2) an infant	(b) having a big effect
(3) impressive	(c) a child
(4) hygiene	(d) independent

A	B
(1) have an impact on	(a) to reproduce/copy
(2) to replicate	(b) a link
(3) a connection	(c) the things you study on a course
(4) the curriculum	(d) have an effect on

Test Book 6

Reading Test 4, Reading Passage 2: Do Literate Women make better Mothers?

How to Answer Questions 27 to 30:

With these "matching paragraphs and headings" questions, you have to find the main idea of a paragraph and match it to a heading. Sometimes, you can get the answer from the topic sentence of the paragraph, which is often -- but not always -- the first sentence in the paragraph. Try to do this first. In this test, you can get the answers to questions 28 and 30 from the first sentence. Do not forget to read the rest of the paragraph to confirm that your answer is correct. With the other questions, you need to read the whole paragraph. One way of doing this is to read the paragraph and think of your own heading, and then try to match it with a heading in the questions.

Do not forget to look for synonyms and paraphrases. For example, what words in the headings have a similar meaning to the word "change" in the first sentence of paragraph D? "Matching paragraphs and headings" questions are normally the first questions on the list. Often, but not always, the first questions after that will relate to the first part of the text, and the final questions to the end of the text. This is the case in this test.

Now, answer questions 27 to 30.

How to Answer Questions 31 to 34:

These are "multiple choice" questions. These questions, in this particular test, relate to the first four paragraphs of the text. Multiple choice questions are always in the same order as the text.

Look for words, especially proper nouns, in the stems of the questions that may be the same as in the text. Additionally, look for synonyms and paraphrases.

Possible Strategies for Answering Questions 31 to 34: You could just read the stem of the question, read the text and try to complete the sentence in your own words. You could then try to match your sentence with an option. Or, you could try to guess the correct answer and then read the text to see if you are right. Finally, you could, of course, read all the options before you look at the text, and then read the text to find the correct option.

Question 31
The answer to the first question is often near the start of the text. Find the words "survey"and "secondaryschools"and underline them. Read the information before and after the words carefully, and answer the question.

Question 32
The phrase "There is no bullying at this school"is a quote from the text, so you will be able to find the exact words in the text. Find them in paragraph three and underline them. Read the information carefully, and answer the question.

Question 33
The phrase "There is no bullying at this school"is a quote from the text, so you will be able to find the exact words in the text. Find them in paragraph three and underline them. Read the information carefully, and answer the question.

Question 34
Find the word "Norway"in paragraph four of the text and underline it. Then, read the information before and after it carefully, and answer the question.
After you have answered the questions, match the phrases in the questions in column A, below, with similar ones in the text in Column B to help you check that your answers are correct.

A	B
(1) lack of knowledge	(a) was halved
(2) little help was available	(b) difficulties with interpersonal relationships
(3) difficulty forming relationships	(c) as adults
(4) later in life	(d) not much was known
(5) declined by 50%	(e) lack of resources

How to Answer Questions 31 to 34:

These are "summary completion" questions in which you need to complete the summary with words from the text. The answers will relate to only a part of the text. As they are at the end, it is likely they will relate to the final part of the text. This is the case in this example. All of the answers can be found in paragraph E.

Read through the summary to make sense of it, and predict what type of words are missing. The missing words are:

Question 35
a singular noun

Question 36
a plural or uncountable noun

Question 37
How is the second theory signposted? It is signposted with the words "**another hypothesis**". The synonym for "focus on" in the text is "**emphasizes**".

Question 38
a plural or uncountable noun

Question 39
Sometimes, the words in the summary and the text will be the same. For example, for question 37, the words "through the" are the same in the question and the text. More often, however, you will need to find synonyms and paraphrases in the text that have the same meaning as words in the summary. Do not forget to check how many words you can use. Answer questions 35 to 39, and check your answers by matching the words in column A with their synonyms and paraphrases in column B, below.

A	B
(1) the most important step	(a) explicit
(2) produce	(b) distinguish
(3) detailed	(c) who are liable to be
(4) potential	(d) a key step
(5) recognise the difference	(e) develop

Question 40

Question 40 is a "global question". You need to decide on the best title for the whole text.

Test Book 6

Reading Test 4, Reading Passage 3: Bullying At School

Match the words and phrases from the text in column A with their definitions in column B.

A	B
(1) to shove	(a) to push
(2) persistent	(b) very unhappy
(3) depressed	(c) how bad something is
(4) the severity	(d) lasting a long time

A	B
(1) recalcitrant	(a) to do something about a problem
(2) to tackle	(b) a collection of material
(3) a pack	(c) to make less
(4) to reduce	(d) difficult to get rid of

A	B
(1) explicit	(a) when things are clean
(2) a sanction	(b) having a big effect
(3) a consultation	(c) a child
(4) the curriculum	(d) independent

A	B
(1) to blame	(a) to recognise the difference
(2) to distinguish	(b) to accuse somebody of doing something bad
(3) substantial	(c) a goal
(4) an objective	(d) significant, more than a little

Tips for the Listening Exam

In order to do well in the listening exam, you need to listen to as much English as possible outside the classroom. Below are a few hints that should help you when you take the listening component of the IELTS Exam. You should "practice" performing these actions when you are taking the practice exams so that these behaviours become automatic long before taking the actual IELTS Exam.

- Take all the time available to read the questions before doing the listening. When you are told that you have 30 seconds to review your answers, you should, instead, read the questions in the next section.
- Try to predict what types of words are missing, using your knowledge of English grammar. For example, if the word follows a preposition, the missing word will be either a noun or a gerund.
- Sometimes, you will be able to guess the exact word. In "sentence completion" questions, you should use the context to try to guess exactly what the word might be.
- At the end of the exam, you should check to ensure that youhave not left any questions unanswered. If you do not know an answer, just guess! You will notlose any marks for an incorrect answer. If you leave an answer blank, you get no points for that answer. Similarly, if you answer the question incorrectly, you will get no points. However, if you answer correctly, even by guessing, you will get points for that answer.
- You must stay focused and concentrate when taking these exams. You should try not to lose your place and should follow the order of the questions closely. Do not let your mind wander. You will not find the answers on the ceiling or out the window.
- Remain calm during the exam. Donot panic. If you feel that you have missed an answer, do not worry or start to panic. Just move on to the next question. If you dwell on an answer that you have missed, you might miss a couple of easy questions further ahead in the exam.
- Sometimes, two answers might come very close together and then there might be a long gap before the next question. You need to be aware of this.
- The questions at the beginning of the listening exam will be easier than those at the end of the exam.
- If you have to spell a name or write down a telephone number, you should do this immediately, as it probably will not be repeated.
- Just because you hear a word in the listening that matches an answer on the question paper, does not necessarily mean that that word is the correct answer. In fact, theymay be trying to "catch you out". It is much more likely that you will hear a synonym or a parallel expression than it is that you will hear the exact word written on the question paper. This is especially true towards the end of the exam, where hearing the exact words on the listening as are on the question paper may indicate that the answer is wrong.

IELTS Academic Listening Exam - Question Types

There are a variety of question types in the listening test. All questions are in the same order as the information in the recording. The question types include:

1. Multiple choice
2. Short answer
3. Sentence completion
4. Labeling a map/diagram/plan
5. Form/note/table/flow chart/summary completion
6. Matching

Test Book 6

Test book 6 - Listening Test 1: Synonyms and Parallel Expressions

Can you remember the synonyms and parallel expressions used in the listening test? Try to complete the missing words and phrases, and then listen to the listening again to check that you were right.

Words on the question paper	Words on the question paper
(Q7) from.......to	b_t_e_n / a_d
(Q13) reduced in number	a_e / n_w / f_w_r
(Q21) attend a class	s_t / i_ / o_ / a_t_a_h_n_ / s_s_i_n
(Q22) inform them	w_r_ / t_e / r_f_c_o_y
(Q24) reduced	l_s_ / t_a_
(Q31) produce (noun)	c_o_s / a_d / l_v_s_o_k
(Q31) was used to	h_l_e_ / t_
(Q31) the people of London	t_a_ / p_p_l_t_o_
(Q32) new technology	t_e / technology / t_e_ / i_t_o_u_e_ f_w_r
(Q33) lack of	ships/ w_r_ / c_n_t_u_t_d
(Q34) for the building of ships	t_e / r_s_ / o_ / England
(Q35) other parts of England	e_t_e_e / poverty
(Q37) great poverty	v_r_ / b_d_y / b_i_t
(Q 38 - 40) poor standards of building	c_o_d_d / c_o_e_y /
(Q 38 - 40) overcrowding	t_g_t_e_
(Q 38 - 40) overcrowding	A / t_n_ / d_m_ / u_h_a_t_y / h_u_e / l_k_ / t_i_ / m_g_t / w_l_ / b_ / o_c_p_e_ / b_ / t_o / f_l_ / f_m_l_e_ /

Test Book 6

Listening Test 2: Synonyms and Parallel Expressions

Can you remember the synonyms and parallel expressions used in the listening test? Try to complete the missing words and phrases, and then listen to the listening again to check that you were right.

Words on the question paper	Words in the listening
(Q1) under	b _ l _ w
(Q3) push	p _ e _ s
(Q4) behind	a _ / t _ e / b _ c _ / o f
(Q5) by phoning	b _ / c _ l _ i _ g
(Q7) children	k _ d _
(Q13) depart	l _ a _ e
(Q14) includes refreshments	refreshments / a _ e / i _ c _ u _ e _
(Q17) seat reservations essential	y _ u / h _ v _ / t _ / m _ k _ / seat / reservations
(Q21) read IT catalogues	l _ o _ / t _ r _ u _ h / catalogues / s _ e _ i _ l _ s _ n _ / i _ / IT
(Q23) prepare a checklist for the survey	d _ a _ / u _ / a / survey / checklist d _ d _ 't / m _ n _ g _ / t _ / g _ t /
(Q25) couldn't find the essays on	h _ l _ / o _ / t _ e / essays / a _ o _ t
(Q28) include more references to works dated after	Y _ u / s _ o _ l _ / a _ m / t _ / c _ t _ / m _ r _ / w _ r _ s / w _ i _ t _ n / l _ t _ r / t _ a _
(Q30) before starting on the research	b _ f _ r _ / y _ u / e _ b _ r _ / u _ o _ / the / research
(Q32) available technology	e _ i _ t _ n _ / technology
(Q33) very heavy	w _ i _ h _ d / o _ e _ / 200 / k _ l _ g _ a _ s

(Q34) been told about	h _ a _ d / a _ o _ t
(Q37) removing tension	t _ i _ / t _ o _ / a _ l / the / tension / a _ a _
(Q38) the first motion picture	t _ e / v _ r _ / f _ r _ t / m _ v _ e
(Q39) were used for the first time	w _ r _ / f _ r _ t / u _ e _

Test Book 6

Listening Test 3: Synonyms and Parallel Expressions

Can you remember the synonyms and parallel expressions used in the listening test? Try to complete the missing words and phrases, and then listen to the listening again to check that you were right.

Words on the question paper	Words in the listening
(Q3) current address	w _ e _ e / a _ e / y _ u / l _ v _ n _ ?
(Q4) current address	p _ e _ e _ t / address
(Q5) telephone - work	d _ y _ i _ e / t _ l _ p _ o _ n _ / n _ m _ e _
(Q8) €2000 to be transferred	I' _ / g _ i _ g / t _ / t _ a _ s _ e _ / €2000
(Q9) every month	o _ c _ e / a / month
(Q10) supply information about	s _ n _ / y _ u / information / about
(Q11) was unsure	w _ s / t _ o / s _ o _ / m _ k _ n _ / u _ / h _ s / m _ n _
(Q13) a typical building of the region	a / p _ r _ / e _ a _ p _ e / o _ / a / t _ a _ i _ i _ n _ l / c _ u _ t _ y / h _ u _ e / o _ / t _ i _ / p _ r _ / o _ / E _ g _ a _ d
(Q18) walk through the field	c _ o _ s / the / field
(Q19) go over the footbridge	c _ o _ s / the / footbridge
(Q20) go up to the viewpoint	c _ i _ b / u _ / t _ / the / viewpoint
(Q21) investigate	l _ o _ / a _
(Q22) must use	h _ v _ / t _ / d _
(Q23) in total	a _ t _ g _ t _ e _
(Q25/26) music preferences	t _ e / k _ n _ / o _ / music / t _ e _ / l _ k _

(Q28) source of music	w_e_e/t_e_/a_t_a_l_/g_t/ t_e_r/m_s_c
(Q31) come from	t_e/o_i_i_s
Q32) above	e_c_e_e_
Q33) have limited the distance	h_v_/s_v_r_l_/r_s_r_c_e_/ t_e/r_n_e
(Q34) marks	i_p_e_s_o_s
(Q35) pulled by	d_a_n/b_
(Q36) water and sand were necessary	t_e_/n_e_e_/ water / and / sand
(Q38) to make them watertight	t_/r_t_i_/w_t_r
(Q40) the earliest	a_/f_r_t

Test Book 6

Listening Test 4: Synonyms and Parallel Expressions

Can you remember the synonyms and parallel expressions used in the listening test? Try to complete the missing words and phrases, and then listen to the listening again to check that you were right.

Words on the question paper	Words in the listening
(Q2) payment by cheque	s _ n _ / a / cheque / t _ / u _
(Q5) approximately	a _ o _ t
(Q5) from Conference Centre	f _ o _ / h _ r _
(Q11) checking the entrance tickets	s _ a _ p _ n _ / the / entrance / tickets
(Q13) car park traffic	t _ e / t _ a _ f _ c / i _ / t _ e / c _ r / p _ r _ s
(Q14) give out the tax forms	h _ n _ i _ g / o _ t / y _ u _ / tax / forms
(Q15) explain about	g _ / t _ r _ u _ h
Q18) video title	a / video / c _ l _ e _
(Q21) a variety of	a / r _ n _ e / o _
(Q23) the majority of	m _ s _ / o _
(Q24) resources	m _ t _ r _ a _
(Q25) are only available at	y _ u 'l _ / n _ e _ / t _ / u _ e
(Q27) recalled	r _ q _ e _ t _ d / b _ / a _ o _ h _ r / b _ r _ o _ e _
(Q28-30) making good use of	h _ w / t _ / u _ e
Q28-30) using the Internet	o _ l _ n _
(Q28-30) standard requirements when writing a dissertation	a _ a _ e _ i _ / w _ i _ i _ g / c _ n _ e _ t _ o _ s
(Q32) pictures	i _ a _ e _ s
(Q33) disappeared from Europe	Europe / s _ w / i _ s / l _ s _
(Q34) very few	n _ t / m _ n _
(Q36) threat	d _ n _ e _

(Q37) protected by	s _ v _ d / b _
(Q38) consists of	i _ / m _ d _ / u _ / o _
(Q39) when water is short	i _ / t _ m _ s / o _ / d _ o _ g _ t

Tips for the Listening Exam
- Read the instructions carefully and make sure you understand what they say.
- Always spend time planning your essay and brainstorming ideas before beginning to write.
- Practice writing within the time limit and **wear a watch to the exam**. Students often run out of time and do not write enough words. You must write at least the minimum number of words. If you do not, you will lose a large number of marks.
- You may want to consider which writing task (Task 1 or Task 2) you are more comfortable with, and answer that question FIRST, before answering the question you find more difficult. If you do not understand the question in Task 2, or it looks particularly difficult, it might be best to do Task 1 first. However, make sure that you spend no more than 20 minutes on Task 1 and 40 minutes on Task 2. Also, consider that Task 2 is worth twice as much as Task 1; therefore, you might consider completing Task 2 first for this reason.
- One way to improve your writing, in general, is to read many easy books, such as "Easy Readers".``
- Use a wide range of grammatical structures and use accurate grammar.
- Also, use a wide range of advanced vocabulary. Try not to repeat the same words.
- Use appropriate paragraphing and linking/transition words.
- Do not use contractions. There are two reasons not to use contractions. First, not using them is more formal, and this is an academic writing exam. Second, by not using contractions, you are increasing the number of words: contractions count as one word, not using them counts as two words.
- Although you need to concentrate on the main points (e.g., the main trends or differences), it is important that you mention every item in the graph, process diagram, or map. For example, if there are five countries in the graph, you should mention all of them.
- Leave some time at the end of the exam to check your writing for sense, tense, and grammatical errors.

Writing Assessment Criteria
There are four things that an examiner takes into consideration when deciding what score to give you on the writing portion of the exam. They are:
- Task achievement/response - Is your response accurate and relevant, and did you meet the minimum number of words for Task 1 (150 words) and Task 2 (250 words).
- Coherence and cohesion - How clear and fluid is your writing, and how have you organised information and ideas in your response; have you used linking words, pronouns, and conjunctions so that the reader can easily understand your response.
- Range of vocabulary and accuracy/appropriateness of use.
- Grammatical range and accuracy.

Writing Task 1

- You should have familiarised yourself with and have had a lot of practice in answering the different possible question types for Writing Task 1. You will usually have to describe a graph, a process, a table, how something works, or you will have to compare two maps.
- In general, there are three parts to a Writing Task 1 response: 1) Introduce the graph/process diagram/table/maps, 2) Give an overview, 3) Give the main details.
- Make sure you begin with an introduction that briefly indicates what the graph, process diagram, table, or maps show - the main idea of the graph, process diagram, table, or maps. Also, say what the main changes, differences, or points are. You can begin with the word "Overall". Use the information in the graph, process diagram, table, or maps and paraphrase the question to help form your opening sentence.
- If appropriate, take into consideration the time period reflected by the graph/process diagram/table/maps, and/or the units of measurement or subjects that are being used and refer to these/use these expressions, measurements, or subjects in your written response.
- Only describe what you can see. Do not give reasons or opinions in this part of the writing exam.
- If you are describing a graph, think about whether you need to use language to compare and contrast and to describe changes over time. Make sure you can use comparatives, superlatives, and language to describe change. Use a variety of structures. For example, when describing changes you could say "Prices increased dramatically" (noun + verb + adverb) or "There was a dramatic increase in prices" (There + be + a/an + adjective + noun + in + noun).
- When describing graphs or maps that reflect changes over time, make sure that you use the correct tenses. For example, if you are referring to a finished period of time, use the past simple. If you are referring to a time period that extends into the future, you can use "will"+ infinitive.
- Use appropriate linking words, such as "whereas" and "in contrast," to make comparisons between things when describing the graphs or the maps.
- The number of paragraphs you will need to write depends on the question. It is, however, a good idea to write a conclusion, which summarises the main points, especially if you haven't written enough words.
- Make sure that you have written at least 150 words.
- If you have to describe a process, you should use the passive as well as the active. Make sure you become adept at using it.
- Make sure that you include all the information in your part one answer. For example, if the graph shows five countries, you should mention all of those countries.

Writing Task 2

- In Writing Task 2, you will have to write some type of essay. It is often, but not always, an opinion essay, but it could also be, for example, a "problem-solution" essay or a "for-and-against" essay. Make sure that you are familiar with the different possible essay types.
- Make sure that you use appropriate paragraphing and that it is clear where the paragraphs begin and end.
- Check to see that each paragraph has an appropriate topic sentence to introduce it.
- Ensure that you have an introduction that discusses the question and tells the reader what your essay is going to be about.
- Every essay should have a conclusion in which you summarise the main points and give your opinion. Make sure that you use an appropriate phrase such as "In conclusion," to introduce your conclusion. In addition, make sure that you use an appropriate phrase such as "I strongly believe that" to introduce your opinion. Additionally, make sure that you leave enough time to write a conclusion.
- Use appropriate linking words such as "For example", "As a result", "However","Because", "On the other hand", and "For this reason", to link your ideas together.
- Give lots of reasons and examples to justify your arguments.
- Also, it is a good idea to discuss both sides of an argument to give balance. You can always refute (say why you think the other argument is wrong) before you give your opinion.
- Make sure that you have written at least 250 words and that you have answered the question!
- Use hedging words such as "most", and "usually" to ensure that what you say is actually true.

Tips for the Speaking Exam

- Smile and maintain eye contact with the examiner at appropriate times.
- Give extended responses to answers with lots of reasons and examples.
- Work on your pronunciation, as this is assessed in the exam.
- Try to keep speaking naturally and without pausing, as fluency is one of the criteria assessed. Do not speak too quickly, nor to slowly, but at a natural speed.
- Work on your grammar before the exam, as the use of a wide range of structures and accuracy will increase your score.
- Try to use an advanced level and range of vocabulary.
- Practice asking and answering questions with your friends in your free time. Record yourself and listen to your answers, taking notes on any errors you made and/or what you might have done differently.
- Use fillers such as "of course", "you know", "actually", and "in fact", so that you sound more natural and coherent.
- As in the writing exam, try to use appropriate linking words to link your ideas together.

Speaking Assessment Criteria

There are four things that an examiner thinks about when deciding what score to give you on the speaking portion of the exam. They are:

- Fluency and coherence - How clear and fluid is your speech, and how have you organised information and ideas in your responses; have you used linking words, pronouns, and conjunctions so that the listener can easily understand your response.
- Range of vocabulary and accuracy/appropriateness of use
- Grammatical range and accuracy
- Pronunciation

Part 1

- The examiner will begin by asking you about either your hometown or your studies, if you are a student, or your work, if you have a job. These questions are designed to put you at ease before continuing on with the rest of the speaking exam.
- He or she will then ask you questions on familiar topics.
- Do not forget to give extended answers, not just one word responses.

Part 2

- In this part of the exam, you will be given a card with a topic on it that you will have to speak about for between one and two minutes. There will be four points on the card that you should mention: make sure you speak about each of these points.
- You will be given one minute (and some paper and a pencil) to make some notes before the exam begins.
- When you practice, try to keep speaking for at least two minutes. Do not worry if the examiner stops you after two minutes, but make sure that you have mentioned all the points on the card.
- Do not write complete sentences in your notes but just words and phrases. Also, make a note of any relevant vocabulary that you know which might impress the examiner.
- The examiner will normally ask one or two follow-up questions when you have finished speaking. These are "bridging" questions, as they will lead into Part 3 of the speaking exam.
- Think about which tense you need to use and which structures would be appropriate before and while you are speaking.

Part 3

- In this part of the exam, the examiner will ask you questions about more abstract issues, based on the topic in Part 2.
- Once again, give extended responses to the questions with lots of reasons and examples.
- Use appropriate expressions to introduce your opinions, such as "I think that", "I tend to think that", "I strongly believe that", and "It seems to me that".
- Do not panic! If you do not understand the question, you can ask the examiner to rephrase it. Say, "Could you rephrase that, please?" The examiner will then rephrase the question.

Answer Key – Book 6

Test Book 6
Reading Test 1, Reading Passage 1: Australia's Sporting Success
Questions 1 to 7- Synonyms and Paraphrases Match

(1)	(c)	(1)	(a)
(2)	(b)	(2)	(c)
(3)	(a)	(3)	(b)
(4)	(e)		
(5)	(d)		

Question 1
The answer is paragraph B. The word "sports" is mentioned in this paragraph, as are the words "sports scientists" and "doctors", who are people that have "expertise". The key sentence is the third sentence.

Question 2
The answer is paragraph C. The paraphrase of "visual imaging" is "images from digital cameras".

Question 3
The answer is paragraph B again. The quote in the last sentence of the paragraph tells us that some areas of research useful are not.

Question 4
The answer is paragraph F. The synonym for "reproduced" is "copying".

Question 5
The answer is paragraph D. The word "optimum" means the best possible. Factors such as "heart rate", "sweating", and "heat production" can "have an impact on an athlete's ability to run", as can "coughs" and "colds". We are also told that if a swimmer can "improve on his turns, he can do much better".

Question 6
The answer is paragraph A. The organisations are the AIS and the ASC. The latter "finances programmes... for thousands of sportsmen and women". In other words, it "funded ... athletes".

Question 7
The answer is paragraph B. The word "sports" is mentioned in this paragraph, as are the words "sports scientists" and "doctors", who are people that have "expertise". The key sentence is the third sentence.

Question 8
The answer is paragraph C. The paraphrase of "visual imaging" is "images from digital cameras".

Question 9
The answer is paragraph B again. The quote in the last sentence of the paragraph tells us that some areas of research useful are not.

Question 10
The answer is paragraph F. The synonym for "reproduced" is "copying".

Question 11
The answer is paragraph D. The word "optimum" means the best possible. Factors such as "heart rate", "sweating", and "heat production" can "have an impact on an athlete's ability to run", as can "coughs" and "colds". We are also told that if a swimmer can "improve on his turns, he can do much better".

Question 12
The answer is paragraph A. The organisations are the AIS and the ASC. The latter "finances programmes... for thousands of sportsmen and women". In other words, it "funded ... athletes".

Question 13
The answer is paragraph A. The organisations are the AIS and the ASC. The latter "finances programmes... for thousands of sportsmen and women". In other words, it "funded ... athletes".

Vocabulary from Reading Test 1, Reading Passage 1

(1)	(d)	(1)	(d)	(1)	(b)	(1)	(c)
(2)	(c)	(2)	(a)	(2)	(c)	(2)	(d)
(3)	(a)	(3)	(b)	(3)	(a)	(3)	(b)
(4)	(b)	(4)	(c)	(4)	(d)	(4)	(a)

Test Book 6
Reading Test 1, Reading Passage 2: Australia's Sporting Success

Question 14
The answer is I. It is possible that the author might make a suggestion in the conclusion of the article when he or she is summing up. The words "would help" suggest that it is a good thing to do. The phrase "help the world's economies grow even closer" means the same as "improving trade".

Question 15
The answer is F. The "computer software" can be exported electronically by "transmitting it over telephone lines". The "effects" of this are then listed at the end of the paragraph.

Question 16
The answer is E. The synonym of "local" is "domestic". The "cost" will be "similar" as they "will not face hugely bigger freight bills".

Question 17
The answer is D. The phrase with a similar meaning to "the value of goods" is "goods whose worth". Notice that the word "goods" is the same in the question and the text. The last sentence in the paragraph confirms that you have the correct paragraph.

Question 18
The answer is "True". The sentence has the same meaning as the sentence in the questions.

Question 19
The answer is "False". The controlling word in the statement is "guarantees". The fact that "trade may lose its advantages" means that "effective trade conditions" cannot be guaranteed.

Question 20
The answer is "Not Given". It is the agricultural and manufacturing sectors of the economy which are greater in France than Japan. Although the words "meat" and "steel" are mentioned, we are given no information with regard to which countries import the most.

Question 21
The answer is "True". The two phrases have the same meaning.

Question 22
The answer is "Not Given". The country "Germany" is not mentioned anywhere in the text.

Question 23

The answer is G - trade. The relevant information is in paragraph G. "Technological innovations" or "modern cargo handling methods" led to "swift productivity improvements in cargo handling". This "streamlining" meant that "thousands of boxes at a time could be moved". In other words, it has "had a significant effect on trade".

Question 24

The answer is B - components. You need to go back to paragraph E to find the answer to this question. The words "domestic market" correspond to the words "local supplier" and "drives" are "components" of a computer.

Question 25

The answer is C – container ships. The relevant information is in paragraph G. Before containerisation, the goods transported could be "damaged" or "stolen". After, by implication, they could be moved "safely" and "efficiently" ("thousands of boxes at a time").

Question 26

The answer is A – tariffs. Tariffs are a tax on imports and exports. The relevant information is in paragraphs H and I. The "domestic cargo sector" refers to goods being transported within the country, such as by "road hauliers" and "railways".

Vocabulary from Reading Test 1, Reading Passage 2

(1)	(d)	(1)	(a)	(1)	(b)	(1)	(a)
(2)	(a)	(2)	(c)	(2)	(a)	(2)	(d)
(3)	(c)	(3)	(d)	(3)	(d)	(3)	(c)
(4)	(b)	(4)	(b)	(4)	(c)	(4)	(b)

Test Book 6
Reading Test 1, Reading Passage 3: Climate Change and the Inuit

Question 27
The answer is i. The words "climate change" are the same in the heading and the text. The "reaction" of the Innuit to climate change is to combine "their ancestral knowledge with the best of modern science".

Question 28
The answer is vi. The topic sentence describes "a difficult landscape". The word "hardships" in the second sentence also tells us that it is "difficult" as do the phrases "meagre pickings" and "tested them to the limits".

Question 29
The answer is iii. The "essential supplies" are "food and clothing". Instead of being produced locally, they are flown in or brought in by ship.

Question 30
The answer is vii. Another word for an "effect" is an "impact". "Obesity", "heart disease", "diabetes", "a crisis of identity" and "depression" are all ""negative effects on well-being".

Question 31
The answer is iv. We are told that "Western scientists" are "starting to draw on" the "wisdom" of the Inuits. In other words, they are starting to "respect" it. The words "credibility" and "weight" also imply "respect".

Question 32
The answer is ii. The key phrases in the paragraph are "There are still huge gaps in our environmental knowledge" and "many predictions are no more than best guesses".

Question 33
The answer is "farming". The words "Canadian Arctic" in paragraph C are the same in the summary. This will be where the answer is. As "in" is a preposition, we know we are looking for a noun or gerund. The words "is out of the question" correspond with the words "be impossible". We are told that "farming is out of the question", so it would be "impossible for people to engage in farming".

Questions 33 to 40 - Synonyms and Paraphrases Match

(1)	(e)	(4)	(d)
(2)	(a)	(5)	(f)
(3)	(b)	(6)	(c)

Question 34-35
The answers are "sea mammals" and "fish". The words "4,500 years ago" relate to the words "for thousands of years', and the phrase "surviving by exploiting" corresponds to the phrase "rely on catching".

Question 36
The answer is "Thule". The word "latter" in the summary refers back to the people who were "successful". The Thule were successful as they were "uniquely well adapted to cope with the Arctic environment". As a result, "the environment did not prove unmanageable".

Question 37
The answer is "islands". The word "Nunavat" in paragraph D is the same in the text and the summary. This is where the answer is. The words "rock" and "ice" are also the same in the text. The phrase "a handful of" relates to the words "a few" in the summary.

Question 38
The answer is "nomadic". The phrase "Over the past 40 years" corresponds to "In recent years", "abandoned" relates to "give up", and "ways" is similar to "lifestyle".

Question 39
The answer is "nature". In the text we have "food and clothing", whereas in the summary we have "food and clothes". The phrase "rely heavily on" is similar to "depend mainly on" in the summary.

Question 40
The answer is "Imported". The word "meat" is a type of "produce", and the fact that it "would cost a family around £7,000 a year" to replace the meat they hunted with imported meat tells us that it is "particularly expensive".

Vocabulary from Reading Test 1, Reading Passage 3

(1)	(d)	(1)	(a)	(1)	(d)	(1)	(a)
(2)	(c)	(2)	(c)	(2)	(c)	(2)	(b)
(3)	(a)	(3)	(d)	(3)	(b)	(3)	(d)
(4)	(b)	(4)	(b)	(4)	(a)	(4)	(c)

Test Book 6
Reading Test 2, Reading Passage 1: Advantages of Public Transport
Questions 1 to 5- Synonyms and Paraphrases Match

(1)	(c)
(2)	(a)
(3)	(b)

Question 1
The answer is ii. If something is "democratic", people have the power to vote and elect their representatives. Similarly, a referendum is a vote by the people on a particular issue.

Question 2
The answer is vii. The phrase "make commuting times far higher" corresponds with the words "increases in travelling time".

Question 3
The answer is iv. The words "increasing wealth" correspond to "higher incomes", and the phrase "where cars are the only viable transport" suggests that there will be more cars. The words "refutes that" in the second sentence tells us that this "need not mean" that.

Question 4
The answer is i. If everyone was pushed into the city centre, it would become overcrowded. The report found that this was "not the best approach" and should, therefore, "be avoided".

Question 5
The answer is iii. The word "together" is the same in the text and in the heading. The research shows that "it is valuable to place people working in related fields together". If "people come together face-to-face", "creativity flourishes", which is a "benefit".

Question 6
The answer is "False". The ISTP study compared "thirty-seven cities around the world", not "every city of the world".

Question 7
The answer is "True". Professor Peter Newman pointed out that "efficient cities" created "a better place to live". In other words, "the quality of life for their inhabitants" would be improved.

Question 8
The answer is "Not Given". The words "tram network" are the same in the question and the text. Although we are told that they have made car use "much lower" in the inner cities, we are not told if they have made it "dangerous for car drivers".

Question 9
The answer is "False". It is "the inner suburbs" that have witnessed an "explosion in demand for accommodation", not the "outer suburbs".

Question 10
The answer is "True". The words "bicycle" and "efficient" are the same in the text and the question. Amsterdam and Copenhagen which have a lot of bicycles were "very efficient", even though their public transport systems were only "reasonable but not special". In other words, they were "only averagely good".

Question 11
The answer is F. The city Perth is mentioned in the second paragraph. It has "limited" or "minimal" public transport. As a result, it has to spend a large proportion of its wealth on transport costs and is, therefore, inefficient.

Question 12
The answer is D. Auckland is mentioned in the seventh paragraph. It would be "hard" for Auckland "to develop a really good rail network" as it is ""hilly". It is, therefore, "inappropriate". Notice that in the text the words "rail network" are used, whereas in the question it says "rail transport system".

Question 13
The answer is C. Portland is mentioned in the eighth paragraph. Notice that the words "light rail" are the same in the text and the question. They decided to spend money on "light rail" instead of a "new road". This worked "spectacularly well". In other words, it was profitable.

Vocabulary from Reading Test 2, Reading Passage 1

(1)	(d)	(1)	(a)	(1)	(d)	(1)	(b)
(2)	(a)	(2)	(c)	(2)	(a)	(2)	(d)
(3)	(c)	(3)	(d)	(3)	(c)	(3)	(a)
(4)	(b)	(4)	(b)	(4)	(b)	(4)	(c)

Test Book 6
Reading Test 2, Reading Passage 2: Greying Population Stays in the Pink

Question 14
The answer is B. In the text it says that "the diseases associated with old age are afflicting fewer and fewer people". In other words, "the proportion of people over 65 suffering from the most common age-related medical problems is falling".

Question 15
The answer is I. The answer L "Constant", in fact, would also have fitted. However, we are told that "the rate at which these diseases are declining continues to accelerate." To "accelerate" is to increase.

Question 16
The answer is F. The key sentence is the last sentence in paragraph three. Diseases that in the past affected 65-year-olds are not now affecting people until they are 70 or 75, much "later in life than they did in the past".

Question 17
The answer is M. The key sentence is the first sentence in paragraph four. The words "medical advances" correspond to the words "developments in medicine".

Question 18
The answer is J. The word "nutrition" is actually in the text. In the text we have "improvements in... nutrition", whereas in the summary it says "developments in nutrition".

Question 19
The answer is N. The word "surges" in the first sentence of paragraph five has the same meaning as "increases" in the summary. The increases in some diseases are caused by "poor air quality" or "pollution". The word "pollution" is also in the text.

Question 20
The answer is K. The key sentence is the third sentence in paragraph six. The phrase "life expectancy" refers to how long people can be expected to live.

Question 21
The answer is G. The answer is in paragraph seven. Most people over 65 ("elderly people") could do complex tasks. There were not many "disabled" people in that age group. It represents a "significant drop", which has the same meaning as a "considerable reduction".

Question 22
The answer is A. The answer can be found at the end of paragraph seven. The words "may prove less ... than expected" have the same meaning as "may be less than previously predicted". A "financial burden" is a "cost".

Synonyms and Paraphrases Match

(1)	(f)	(5)	(k)	(9)	(g)
(2)	(d)	(6)	(e)	(10)	(c)
(3)	(h)	(7)	(j)	(11)	(a)
(4)	(b)	(8)	(i)		

Question 23

The answer is G. The key sentence is the first sentence in paragraph eight. In the text, instead of "old people" we have "elderly people", and instead of "independent" we have "self-reliant".

Question 24

The answer is E. The key paragraph is paragraph nine. The word "mental" appears in both the question and the text. The words "physical activity" have the same meaning as "exercise" and the phrase "may prevent the brains of active humans from deteriorating" corresponds to the phrase "may prevent mental decline".

Question 25

The answer is H. The answer can be found in paragraph 10. The word "control" is the same in the text and the question. The answer is not C, as it has an opposite meaning to the text. The words "challenging activities" mean the same as "difficult situations" and the phrase "lower levels of stress hormones" corresponds to the words "reduce stress".

Question 26

The answer is C. The key information is in paragraph 11. The words "emotionally isolated" relate to the words "feelings of loneliness" and the words "higher levels" correspond to the words "rises in levels".

Vocabulary from Reading Test 1, Reading Passage 2

(1)	(d)	(1)	(a)	(1)	(a)	(1)	(c)
(2)	(c)	(2)	(d)	(2)	(d)	(2)	(b)
(3)	(b)	(3)	(b)	(3)	(b)	(3)	(d)
(4)	(a)	(4)	(c)	(4)	(c)	(4)	(a)

Test Book 6
Reading Test 2, Reading Passage 3: Numeration

Synonyms and Paraphrases Match

(1)	(b)
(2)	(c)
(3)	(d)
(4)	(a)

Question 27: The answer is B. The key information is at the end of the second paragraph. The phrase "a sophisticated number system" corresponds to the phrase "a developed system of numbering", the word "began" is the same in the text and the question, and "grow plants and herd animals" relate to "farming".

Question 28: The answer is E. The key information is in paragraph three. The phrase "accompanied by gestures" corresponds to the words "additional hand signals", and the words "were only able to count one, two, many" inform us that "the range of number words was restricted".

Question 29: The answer is A. The key information is in the last sentence of paragraph four. The words "seventh century" and "Europe" are the same in the text and the question. We are told that "people had to be able to count to nine" ("the ability to count to a certain number") in order to "qualify as a witness in a court of law" ("fulfil a civic role").

Question 30: The answer is C. The key information can be found in the first sentence of paragraph five. If something is not a "physical object", it is "an abstract idea". In the text we have the word "developing", whereas in the question we have the word "developed", so the phrase "developing a sense of number" corresponds with the phrase "the development of arithmetic".

Question 31: The answer is G. The key information is in paragraph six. The words "according to class of item" are the same in the question and the text. The phrase "early numeration systems" relates to the words "relics of an older system".

Question 32: The answer is "True". The key information is at the beginning of the second paragraph. The words "earliest tribes" are the same in the question and the text. The question "Is this enough?" relates to "sufficiency", whereas the question "How many?" relates to "quantity".

Question 33: The answer is "False". The key information is in paragraph three. In the question we have "indigenous Tasmanians", while in the text we have "indigenous peoples of Tasmania". They "were only able to count one, two, many". In other words, they used three terms "to indicate numbers of objects", not four.

Question 34: The answer is "True". The key information can be found at the end of paragraph three. They used "gestures" ("body language") "to help resolve any confusion" ("prevent misunderstanding").

Question 35: The answer is "False". The answer can be found at the beginning of paragraph four. The words "cultures" and "large numbers" are the same in the text and the question. The important or "controlling" word in the question is "all". In fact "some" cultures have a "lack of ability" "to deal with large numbers".

Question 36: The answer is "Not Given". The words "Anglo-Saxon" are the same in the question and the text. We are only given the origins of the words "ten" and "hundred", not "thousand".

Question 37: The answer is "True". The key information is can be found at the end of paragraph four. The words "seventh-century" and "Europe" are the same in the question and the text. People had "poor counting ability". They only had to be able to count to nine to be a witness in court, so being able to count to nine was seen as being above average.

Question 38: The answer is "False". The relevant information is in paragraph six. The words "Tsimshian language", "long objects", and "canoes" are all the same in the question and the text. We are told that there are seven classes of items which all have "distinct sets of words" for numbers. They are then listed. We can see that the sets or categories for "long objects" and "canoes" are separate, and, therefore, not the same.

Question 39: The answer is "True. The key sentence is the second last sentence in paragraph six. The word "older" is the same in the question and the text, whereas "later" is a synonym of "newer".

Question 40: The answer is "Not Given". We are told that people used pebbles to count with, but we are not told whether they found it easier to use their fingers.

Vocabulary from Reading Test 2, Reading Passage 3

(1)	(d)	(1)	(a)	(1)	(c)	(1)	(b)
(2)	(c)	(2)	(d)	(2)	(a)	(2)	(a)
(3)	(b)	(3)	(b)	(3)	(b)	(3)	(d)
(4)	(a)	(4)	(c)	(4)	(d)	(4)	(c)

Test Book 6
Reading Test 3, Reading Passage 1: Early Cinema
Synonyms and Paraphrases Match

(1)	(e)
(2)	(d)
(3)	(a)
(4)	(c)
(5)	(b)

Question 1
The answer is A. Instead of "cinema", we have the word "Cinematographe" and the address of the Cinema (14 Boulevard des Capucines in Paris) tells us its "location".

Question 2
The answer is I. The word "stories" is the same in the text and the question. We are told that cinema might have focused on documentaries or become like television, but told "stories" instead. These started as "short stories" and evolved into longer ones.

Question 3
The answer is J. The first sentence has the key information. The phrase "And it has all happened so quickly" corresponds to the phrase "the speed with which cinema has changed".

Question 4
The answer is E. The first and last sentences (the topic and summarising sentences) provide the key information. The word "educate" has the same meaning as "teaches us", and the words "life and values" correspond to the word "culture".

Question 5
The answer is G. The word "star" suggests that we are attracted to actors in films. The words "film personalities" have the same meaning as the words "actors in films", and the expressions "have such an immediate presence", "appear more real to us than we do ourselves", and "The star as magnified human self" all suggest an attraction.

Question 6
The answer is "Yes". The key information is in paragraph B. The phrase "to grasp the impact of those first moving images" corresponds to the phrase "understand how the first audiences reacted to the cinema", while the words "it is worth trying" tell us that it is "important".

Question 7
The answer is "Not Given". The words "one of the greatest" in the text refer to the director, Andrei Tarkovsky, not the film. Although he refers to the film as "a work of genius", we are not told if it was "one of the greatest films ever made".

Question 8
The answer is "Not Given". There is no mention of this in the text.

Question 9
The answer is "No". The key information is in paragraph H. The words "at first" relate to "very early cinema". We are told that at that time all that mattered was "the wonder of movement"- not, therefore, "storylines".

Question 10
The answer is B. The key information is in paragraph C. The audience could not accept that the train was just "pictures". They thought it was real and would move away from the screen because they thought the train "was about to crush them". This shows us what an impact the film had.

Question 11
The answer is C. The key information is in paragraph D. The key phrases are "cinema created a dynamic image of the real flow of events" and "in cinema, the real, objective flow of time was captured".

Question 12
The answer is D. The key information is in paragraph H. The word "began" is the same in the question and the text. At first, "it was by no means obvious how it would be used". In other words, "its future was uncertain".

Question 13
The answer is D. The other options, while mentioned, relate to specific parts of the passage and not its overall meaning.

Vocabulary from Reading Test 3, Reading Passage 1

(1)	(c)	(1)	(d)	(1)	(b)	(1)	(d)
(2)	(b)	(2)	(a)	(2)	(c)	(2)	(a)
(3)	(d)	(3)	(b)	(3)	(a)	(3)	(c)
(4)	(a)	(4)	(c)	(4)	(d)	(4)	(b)

Test Book 6
Reading Test 3, Reading Passage 2: Motivating Employees Under Adverse Conditions

Synonyms and Paraphrases Match

(1)	(e)
(2)	(d)
(3)	(f)
(4)	(c)
(5)	(a)
(6)	(b)

Question 14

The answer is vii. The first, or topic, sentence provides the key information. The word "goals" is similar to the word "targets" and the phrase "receive comments on how well they are doing in those goals" means the same as "give feedback".

Question 15

The answer is iii. If targets are "unachievable", they will not be "realistic" and employees "will reduce their effort". They need to be "realistic". Employees must feel confident that "their efforts can lead to performance goals".

Question 16

The answer is J. The first sentence has the key information. The phrase "And it has The answer is ii. The word "rewards" is the same in the statement and the text. If you "personalise the rewards", you "match rewards to individuals".

Question 17

The answer is iv. The first sentence can give you the answer. Don't forget to read the rest of the paragraph, though, to check that you are correct. If something is "contingent on" something, it is "linked" to it in some way. The word "performance" is related to the word "achievement".

Question 18

The answer is i. Once again, the first sentence contains the key information. The word "equitable" is a synonym of the word "fair". Don't forget to try to guess the meaning of any unknown words from the context. Moreover, if "outcomes... are equal to the inputs given", then they would be "fair".

Question 19
The answer is "No". The word "shrinking" is the same in the question and the text. It is the "best ... workers" who "leave", rather than the "less skilled employees".

Question 20
The answer is "Not Given". In "Key Point One", both "small" and "larger" businesses are mentioned. However, what is mentioned are the different qualities needed by employees for small and large businesses. There is no mention of which is easier to manage.

Question 21
The answer is "No". The key information is in "Key Point One". The words "high achievers" are the same in the question and the text. We are told that high achievers "will do best" where there is "independence": in other words, when they are not working as a team.

Question 22
The answer is "Yes". The words ""goal-setting" can be found in "Key Point Two". The key sentence is the final sentence of the paragraph. Instead of "participate", we have "the participation process" and instead of "manipulated", we have "perceive ... as manipulative".

Question 23
The answer is "Not Given". The words "appraisal process" appear in the last sentence of "Key Point Three". All we are told is that the appraisal process should be seen by employees as valid. There is no mention of whether or not they should design the process.

Question 24
The answer is "Yes". The relevant information is in "Key Point Five". Another word for earnings is "remuneration" and the words "openly communicating" relate to the word "disclosed".

Question 25
The answer is B. The key information is in "Key Point Two". We are told that "high achievers are already internally motivated". In other words, "they have less need of external goals".

Question 26
The answer is C. The words "clerical workers" can be found in "Key Point Six". The word "consider" is similar to the word "think". They "considered factors such as quality of work performed", so "they think the quality of their work is important".

Question 27
The answer is A. The answer can be found in the same paragraph as the answer to the previous question. The word "advancement" is similar to the word "promotion" and the words "rated... very highly" correspond to the words "judge ... to be important".

Synonyms and Paraphrases Match

(1)	(d)
(2)	(b) / (c)
(3)	(a)
(4)	(b) / (c)

Vocabulary from Reading Test 3, Reading Passage 2

(1)	(d)	(1)	(b)	(1)	(d)	(1)	(a)
(2)	(a)	(2)	(a)	(2)	(a)	(2)	(d)
(3)	(b)	(3)	(d)	(3)	(b)	(3)	(b)
(4)	(c)	(4)	(c)	(4)	(c)	(4)	(c)

Test Book 6
Reading Test 3, Reading Passage 3: The Search for the Anti-aging Pill

Question 28
The answer is "No". We are told that "no treatment on the market today" ("drugs available today") "has been proved to slow human aging" ("can delay the process of growing old").

Question 29
The answer is "Yes". "Those findings suggest" ("There is scientific evidence") "that calorific restriction" ("that eating fewer calories") "could ... increase longevity" ("may extend human life").

Question 30
The answer is "Yes". "Few mortals" ("Not many people") "could stick to that harsh a regimen" ("find a caloric-restricted diet attractive"). The words "that harsh a regimen" refer back to the words reducing "their caloric intake by roughly thirty per cent".

Question 31
The answer is "Not Given". It is asked whether people will get fewer age-related illnesses if they eat fewer calories. It does not say whether or not diet-related diseases are common in older people.

Question 32
The answer is "Yes". The key phrase is "rats fed a low-calorie diet lived longer on average than free-feeding rats", which has the same meaning as the statement in the question.

Synonyms and Paraphrases Match

(1)	(d)
(2)	(c)
(3)	(b)
(4)	(a)

Question 33
The answer is "No". We are told that "no treatment on the market today" ("drugs available today") "has been proved to slow human aging" ("can delay the process of growing old").

Question 34
The answer is "Yes". "Those findings suggest" ("There is scientific evidence") "that calorific restriction" ("that eating fewer calories") "could ... increase longevity" ("may extend human life").

Question 35
The answer is C. The word "lifespans" is near the end of paragraph six. This has not been shown yet.

Question 36
The answer is A. The words "heart disease" can be found at the beginning of paragraph six. We are told that "they have lower blood pressure and triglyceride levels (signifying a decreased likelihood of heart disease)". The pronoun "they" refers back to "caloric-restricted animals".

Question 37
The answer is B. The word "insulin" can be found in paragraph five. We can see that "caloric-restricted monkeys... have lower ... levels of ... insulin". Therefore, the control monkeys must have "produced greater quantities of insulin".

Synonyms and Paraphrases Match

(1)	(d)
(2)	(c)
(3)	(a)
(4)	(b)

Question 38
The answer is "glucose". We are told that "the drug prevents most of it from being processed". The pronoun "it" refers back to the word "glucose", so "less glucose is processed".

Question 39
The answer is "free radicals". The key phrase is "limit their production and thereby constrain the damage". The pronoun "their" refers back to the words "free radicals". If the production of free radicals is limited, "fewer free radicals are emitted", and this will "constrain the damage" ("cells less damaged by disease").

Question 40
The answer is "preservation". If "food is scarce" ("food is in short supply"), the cells go into a mode that "emphasizes preservation" ("cells focus on preservation").

Vocabulary from Reading Test 3, Reading Passage 2

(1)	(b)	(1)	(d)	(1)	(a)	(1)	(d)
(2)	(d)	(2)	(c)	(2)	(d)	(2)	(a)
(3)	(a)	(3)	(b)	(3)	(b)	(3)	(b)
(4)	(c)	(4)	(a)	(4)	(c)	(4)	(c)

Test Book 6
Reading Test 4, Reading Passage 1: Doctoring Sales

Question 1
The answer is v. The words "pharmaceutical company" are the same as the words "drug company". The example is the example of the doctor who asks what the representative will give him if he prescribes their drugs. He "expects" to get something from the drug companies.

Question 2
The answer is vi. A number of "gifts" are mentioned such as "a pair of tickets for a New York musical". Two financial gifts are also mentioned: $200 and a "$1,000 honoraria".

Question 3
The answer is iii. The last two lines of the paragraph give you the answer. If you are "to blame for" something, you are "responsible for" it. We also have the noun "responsibility" in the text, instead of the adjective "responsible" in the heading. The phrase "the escalating extravagance of pharmaceutical marketing" corresponds to the phrase "increase in promotion". The word "escalating" means "increasing".

Question 4
The answer is ix. The positive factors listed are: "much-needed information and education"; "sources of drug education for healthcare givers"; and the fact that "salespeople have essentially become specialists in one drug or group of drugs".

Question 5
The answer is i. The key information is at the end of the paragraph. The word "influenced" is a synonym of the word "persuaded".

Question 6
The answer is vii. The word "effective" suggests that it "works". The "study" by the University of Washington" provides evidence to support this.

Question 7
The answer is x. The word "pay" is the same in the text and the heading. We are told that "patients are the ones who pay". The examples of the "doctors' free gifts" in the paragraph are "every pen that's handed out, every free theatre ticket, and every steak dinner eaten".

Synonyms and Paraphrases Match

(1)	(f)
(2)	(d)
(3)	(a)
(4)	(c)
(5)	(g)
(6)	(b)
(7)	(e)

Question 8

The answer is "No". A "budget" is the amount of money you have available to buy something, so "a very limited budget" is different from "a budget that could buy lunches and dinners for a small country". The latter would be a very large budget.

Question 9

The answer is "Yes". The words "moral" and "ethical" have the same meaning. The fact that it is "a daily exercise in ethical judgement" suggests that it "may be open to criticism on moral grounds". Whether the salespeople are paying for the doctors' time or bribing them is a "moral" or "ethical" question.

Question 10

The answer is "No". The word "physician" in the text is another word for a "doctor". The words "much-needed information" have an opposite meaning to the words "information (which) is of little use".

Question 11

The answer is "Yes". The third sentence in Paragraph E gives clear "evidence of drug promotion ... in the healthcare environment".

Question 12

The answer is "Not Given". Although "free samples" are mentioned in the text, there is no mention of whether or not they are given to patients without doctors' prescriptions.

Question 13

The answer is "Yes". In the text, instead of "drug companies" we have "pharmaceutical companies". The author says they "have every right to make a profit". In other words "It is legitimate for drug companies to make money".

Answers to Same/Different

Q8	different
Q9	same
Q10	different
Q13	same

Vocabulary from Reading Test 4, Reading Passage 1

(1)	(a)	(1)	(d)	(1)	(a)	(1)	(d)
(2)	(d)	(2)	(a)	(2)	(d)	(2)	(a)
(3)	(b)	(3)	(b)	(3)	(b)	(3)	(c)
(4)	(c)	(4)	(c)	(4)	(c)	(4)	(b)

Test Book 6
Reading Test 4, Reading Passage 2: Do Literate Women Make Better Mothers?

Question 14
The answer is B (men and women). After "large numbers of" we must have a plural, countable noun. It was "adults" who had learnt to write, so "men and women" is the correct answer.

Question 15
The answer is F (maternal literacy). To find the answer to this question, you need to go back in the text to the first paragraph. The expression "they accepted this idea decades ago", tells us that they " have known for many years". The words "this idea" refers to the fact that children are healthier when their mothers can read and write, and the latter has the same meaning as "maternal literacy"; so there is "a connection between child health and maternal literacy".

Question 16
The answer is C (an international research team). An academic who investigates something is a "researcher". The researchers came from more than one country, so it is an "international research team".

Question 17
The answer is J (family wealth). You need to go back to the second paragraph to find the answer to this question. The other factor is "her family's wealth". The words are almost the same in the text and the question.

Question 18
The answer is F again (maternal literacy). Remember, in the question it says "You may use any letter more than once". Notice that the words "in itself" are the same in the text and the summary. We are told that "a woman's ability to read in itself improves her children's chances of survival". In other words, it is "maternal literacy" which can "improve infant health and survival".

Question 19
The answer is "Not Given". We are told that "some" of the "nearly 3,000 women" who were interviewed "learnt to read as children". We are not told the exact number. Although it might have been "about a thousand" we don't know. Therefore, the answer is "Not Given" rather than "False".

Question 20
The answer is "No". The National Literacy Crusade started in 1979, so the "late 1970s" was before that time. The "infant mortality rate for the children of illiterate mothers was around 110 deaths per thousand', whereas "for women educated in primary school" it was "80 per thousand". Therefore, the information in the text is different from the information in the question.

Question 21
The answer is "Yes". The words "remained ... unchanged" are the same as "stayed at". In the text the words "mortality figures" are used instead of "mortality rates". Before the "Crusade" the "child mortality rate for the illiterate women" was "around 100" and after the "Crusade had ended" it "remained ... unchanged".

Question 22
The answer is C (an international research team). An academic who investigates something is a "researcher". The researchers came from more than one country, so it is an "international research team".

Question 23
The answer is "No". The lowest rate at 80 per thousand was for those women "educated in primary school". The women "who had learnt to read through the campaign (the Crusade)" had a higher rate of "84 per thousand".

Question 24
The answer is "Not Given". We don't know whether or not they were severely malnourished.

Question 25 and 26
The answers are C and E. The first sentence of paragraph ten tells us that B is not a correct option. You should cross out any options which are incorrect. The last two sentences in paragraph eight show that option E is correct, while the information in paragraph nine shows that option C is correct.

Vocabulary from Reading Test 4, Reading Passage 2

(1)	(d)	(1)	(a)	(1)	(d)	(1)	(d)
(2)	(c)	(2)	(d)	(2)	(c)	(2)	(a)
(3)	(a)	(3)	(b)	(3)	(b)	(3)	(b)
(4)	(b)	(4)	(c)	(4)	(a)	(4)	(c)

Test Book 6
Reading Test 4, Reading Passage 3: Bullying at School

Question 27
The answer is iv. The word "survey" can be seen in section A. If you conduct a survey, you carry out "research". The words "British" and "schools" are the same in the text and the heading. The author and his colleague conducted the surveys to see how much bullying there was in British primary and secondary schools. They wanted to see how common it was.

Question 28
The answer is vi. The words and phrases that introduce the effects are "can make", "can... lead to", and "are more likely to".

Question 29
The answer is v. In the past the "reaction from schools" was to deny the problem. Now, they are more likely to admit that there is some bullying and say they have a policy to deal with it.

Question 30
The answer is vii. The first sentence gives you a clue. A "change" is a "new approach" and the "factors" correspond to the "developments". Although you can often get the heading from the topic sentence, it is important that you read the rest of the paragraph to confirm that you are correct.

Question 31
The answer is B. The words "survey" and "secondary schools" can all be found in section A.

Question 32
The answer is D. The effects of bullying can be found in section two. The key phrase is "pupils are more likely to experience difficulties with interpersonal relationships as adults". The words "as adults" mean when they are adults or "later in life".

Question 33
The answer is D. This is quite tricky and you may well have selected option A. It is incorrect, however, as the saying is no longer true in "more" schools than before. It does not necessarily mean that it is not true in "many" schools". In fact, you need to look at section four to find the answer. The words "this change" in the first sentence of section D refer to the fact that less schools now deny that there is bullying in their school. This is because they have a better "awareness" of the problem and "resources" to deal with it now, which, by implication, they didn't have before.

Question 34

The answer is A. After "an intervention campaign" ("an anti-bullying campaign"), "bullying was halved" ("bullying declined by 50%").

Synonyms and Paraphrases Match

(1)	(d)
(2)	(e)
(3)	(b)
(4)	(c)
(5)	(a)

Question 35

The answer is "policy". A "key step" is "an important step", the words "to develop" are similar to the words "to produce", and we have the adverb "clearly" rather than the adjective "clear".

Question 36

The answer is "(explicit) guidelines". The word "occurs" is the same in the text and the summary. The words "what will be done" correspond to the words "how the school and its staff will react".

Question 37

The answer is "(school) curriculum". The preposition "through" is the same in the summary and the text. The words "In addition" relate to the word "other", and the words "early phases of development" are similar to the phrase "the early part of the process".

Question 38

The answer is "victims". The words "who are liable to be" which come before the word "victim" are similar to the word "potential" which comes before the gap in the summary.

Question 39

The answer is "playful fighting". The word "playground" is the same in the text and the summary. The "lunchtime supervisors" are the "members of staff", and the words "distinguish ... from" correspond to the words "recognise the difference between".

Synonyms and Paraphrases Match

(1)	(d)
(2)	(e)
(3)	(a)
(4)	(c)
(5)	(b)

Question 35

The answer is "policy". A "key step" is "an important step", the words "to develop" are similar to the words "to produce", and we have the adverb "clearly" rather than the adjective "clear".

Question 36

The answer is "(explicit) guidelines". The word "occurs" is the same in the text and the summary. The words "what will be done" correspond to the words "how the school and its staff will react".

Question 37

The answer is "(school) curriculum". The preposition "through" is the same in the summary and the text. The words "In addition" relate to the word "other", and the words "early phases of development" are similar to the phrase "the early part of the process".

Question 38

The answer is "victims". The words "who are liable to be" which come before the word "victim" are similar to the word "potential" which comes before the gap in the summary.

Question 39

The answer is "playful fighting". The word "playground" is the same in the text and the summary. The "lunchtime supervisors" are the "members of staff", and the words "distinguish ... from" correspond to the words "recognise the difference between".

Synonyms and Paraphrases Match

(1)	(d)
(2)	(e)
(3)	(a)
(4)	(c)
(5)	(b)

Question 40

The answer is D. The article is mostly concerned with managing and preventing bullying.

Vocabulary from Reading Test 4, Reading Passage 3

(1)	(a)	(1)	(d)	(1)	(d)	(1)	(b)
(2)	(d)	(2)	(a)	(2)	(a)	(2)	(a)
(3)	(b)	(3)	(b)	(3)	(b)	(3)	(d)
(4)	(c)	(4)	(c)	(4)	(c)	(4)	(c)

Test Book 6
Listening Test 1: Synonyms and Parallel Expressions

(Q7)	between … and ….
(Q13)	are now fewer
(Q21)	sit in on teaching session
(Q22)	warn the refectory
(Q24)	less than
(Q31)	crops and livestock
(Q31)	helped to
(Q31)	that population
(Q32)	the technology they introduced
(Q33)	fewer
(Q34)	ships were constructed
(Q35)	the rest of England
(Q37)	extreme poverty
(Q 38-40)	very badly built
(Q38-40)	crowded closely together
(Q38-40)	A tiny, damp, unhealthy house like this might well be occupied by two full families together

Test Book 6
Listening Test 2: Synonyms and Parallel Expressions

(Q1)	below
(Q3)	press
(Q4)	at the back of
(Q5)	by calling
(Q7)	kids
(Q13)	leave
(Q14)	refreshments are included
(Q17)	you have to make seat reservations
(Q21)	look through catalogues specialising in IT
(Q23)	draw up a survey checklist
(Q25)	didn't manage to get hold of the essays about
(Q28)	You should aim to cite more works written later than
(Q30)	before you embark upon the research
(Q32)	existing technology
(Q33)	weighed over 200 kilograms
(Q34)	heard about
(Q37)	this took all the tension away
(Q38)	the very first movie
(Q39)	were first used
(Q40)	to compensate for this poor sound quality

Test Book 6
Listening Test 3: Synonyms and Parallel Expressions

(Q3)	where are you living?
(Q4)	present address
(Q5)	daytime telephone number
(Q8)	I'm going to transfer €2000
(Q9)	once a month
(Q10)	send you information about
(Q11)	was too slow making up his mind
(Q13)	a pure example of a traditional country house of this part of England
(Q18)	cross the field
(Q19)	cross the footbridge
(Q20)	climb up to the viewpoint
(Q21)	look at
(Q22)	have to do
(Q23)	altogether
(Q25/26)	the kind of music they like
(Q28)	where they actually get their music
(Q31)	the origins
(Q32)	exceeded
(Q33)	have severely restricted the range
(Q34)	impressions
(Q35)	drawn by
(Q36)	they needed water and sand
(Q38)	to retain water
(Q40)	at first

Test Book 6
Listening Test 4: Synonyms and parallel expressions

(Q2)	send a cheque to us
(Q5)	about
(Q5)	from here
(Q11)	stamping the entrance tickets
(Q13)	the traffic in the car parks
(Q14)	handing out your tax forms
(Q15)	go through
(Q18)	a video … called
Q21)	a range of
(Q23)	most of
(Q24)	material
(Q25)	you'll need to use
(Q27)	requested by another borrower
(Q28-30)	how to use
(Q28-30)	online
(Q28-30)	academic writing conventions
Q32)	images
(Q33)	Europe saw its last
(Q34)	not many
(Q36)	danger
(Q37)	saved by
(Q38)	is made up of
(Q39)	in times of drought